The
Great
Last Days
Deception

The
Great
Last Days
Deception

Exposing Satan's
New World Order Agenda

J. B. HIXSON

LUCIDBOOKS

The Great Last Days Deception

Copyright © 2012 by J.B. Hixson

Published by Lucid Books in Brenham, TX.
www.LucidBooks.net

First Printing 2012

ISBN-13: 978-1-935909-48-4
ISBN-10: 1935909487

Special Sales: Most Lucid Books titles are available in special quantity discounts. Custom imprinting or excerpting can also be done to fit special needs. Contact Lucid Books at info@lucidbooks.net.

Unless otherwise indicated, all Scripture quotations are taken from the New King James Version.

Table of Contents

Acknowledgements

I would like to thank the following individuals:

Wendy for waking up with me, not only every morning for the last twenty years, but especially over the past few years as the dawn of reality broke through in our lives. I cannot imagine what it would be like to wake up alone in this world (as we now know it).

Bethany, Brooke, Morgan, Landry, Faith, and Abby for patiently tolerating my frequent ad hoc allocutions against Satan's new world order agenda

Mark for his outstanding scholarship, gifted writing ability, and editing skills. His assistance with this manuscript was invaluable. See www.LiteralTruth.org.

Shane whose intelligence, analytical ability, and hours of patient conversation helped me begin to see the world as it really is.

Dennis, Tom, Kurt, and Bruce for sharpening me theologically.

Angie, Barbara, and Caroline for their diligence, time, and expertise in editing this work.

Dedication

This book is dedicated to my parents who taught me to love and pursue Truth even when it is unpopular.

Introduction

For the past several years I have spent a good deal of my time on the road. On average, my speaking schedule has me in thirty to forty states per year. As anyone who travels extensively knows, there are times when the schedule becomes so hectic that you wake up in a hotel room and for the first few moments you are in a daze, struggling to remember where you are. I recall one instance when, after a particularly exhausting day of travel, I was so tired that I slept through my alarm *and* the hotel wake-up call, and came dangerously close to missing my speaking engagement!

Waking up can be difficult, especially when you are excessively tired. But usually, after a hot shower, a cup of coffee, and a little time to get your bearings, you are ready to face the day.

As we look at the world around us, we see a world that is largely asleep. Many people have been so beaten down by the trials and difficulties of life that they have fallen into a lackadaisical, slumbering state of apathy. They go through the motions, blinded to reality, unaware of the many alarms going off around them. This is by design. We have an enemy who desires to blind mankind to the truth (2 Cor. 4:4). He wants us to sleep like children of darkness, unaware of the light all around us (1 Thess. 5:5-6). That is why the Bible warns us to, "be sober, be vigilant; because your adversary the devil walks about like a roaring lion, seeking whom he may devour" (1 Pet. 5:8).

Because we have been lulled to sleep, we often fail to see reality for what it is. We remain ignorant to the fact that things are not always as they appear. This is an important principle that is particularly relevant to the subject matter covered in this book. *Things are not always as they appear.* There are several biblical passages that relate to this principle. For example, "He who answers a matter before he hears it, it is folly and shame to him" (Prov. 18:13). And, "The first one to plead his cause seems right, until his neighbor comes and examines him" (Prov. 18:17). It is the fool who thinks he is right without seeking counsel (Prov. 12:15). "The naive believes everything, but the prudent man considers his steps" (Prov. 14:15, NASB).

In other words, what we see…what we think we know…the reality we have come to accept…does not always represent *true reality*. Things are not always as they appear. There is almost always more to the story. It is seldom about what it appears to be about. Usually, it is about much more than meets the eye. Truth has always been an elusive target. This is especially true in these postmodern times when absolute truth has been abandoned as a philosophical concept altogether. *People are more deceived today than at any other time in human history.* That is why it is imperative that we "examine everything carefully" and "hold fast to that which is good" (1 Thess. 5:21, NASB).

People are more deceived today than at any other time in human history.

In this age of deception, it is more important than ever to look beyond the façade, dig deeper, and search out the truth. We live in an era where "virtual reality" has replaced reality. Image trumps truth. Style supersedes substance. It has become very difficult to separate fact from fiction. As we will see in the pages that follow, this is because Satan, the prince of this world, is a liar and the father of lies. Satan, "was a murderer from the beginning, and does not stand in the truth, because there is no truth in him. When he speaks a lie, he speaks from his own resources, for he is a liar and the father of it" (John 8:44).

As the great deceiver, Satan's primary goal is to blind the hearts of mankind to the truth (2 Cor. 4:4). In this book, we will examine Satan's agenda of deception in great detail. We will learn that his deception has grown more and more powerful with each passing generation (2 Tim. 3:13). The Bible tells us that the age in which we live is an "evil age" where the "whole world is under the sway of the wicked one" (Gal. 1:4; 1 John 5:19). We are facing the great last days deception.

We will trace Satan's agenda from Calvary through the last 2,000 years. We will see how his murderous intention to kill, steal, and destroy all life has gained momentum (John 10:10). It will become clear that the cosmic struggle between good and evil is far more real … far more active than perhaps you ever imagined. The struggles we face are, "not against flesh and blood, but against principalities, against powers, against the rulers of the darkness of this age, against spiritual hosts of wickedness in the heavenly places" (Eph. 6:12).

We also will look at the remedy for deception. We will learn that we must "not sleep, as others do," but "watch and be sober" (1 Thess. 5:6). God has given us the tools we need to stay awake and walk in the light. Once we learn the tactics of Satan, we will be better equipped to recognize his deceptive agenda and confront his lies one by one.

In the chapters that follow, you will be confronted with many truths that are likely to be new to you. Do not become unsettled. Search out the truth. Do the research. Get the whole story before you dismiss these findings. As we have said, waking up is sometimes hard. But the reward is an exciting new day filled with knowledge, and a clearer perspective on life that will help you successfully navigate this present evil age.

Chapter 1

The Day the Lights Went Out

In the beginning was the Word, and the Word was with God, and the Word was God. He was in the beginning with God. All things were made through Him, and without Him nothing was made that was made. In Him was life, and the life was the light of men. And the light shines in the darkness, and the darkness did not comprehend it. - John 1:1-5

It was the darkest hour in human history. The cosmic struggle between good and evil had reached its peak. The events that were about to unfold would shape the future of all mankind.

This powerful battle began before the foundation of the earth. The first attack was an attempt to overcome God Himself. Then, for more than 4,000 years the enemy of righteousness schemed to wrestle control of planet earth from the eternal Creator of the universe. For 4,000 years this adversary worked his deception, blinding human hearts. He was relentless in spite of setbacks, wreaking havoc on the entire world. This fearless enemy was confident that his time had come to defeat God once and for all, or so he thought. In one dark hour ultimate victory seemed within his grasp.

Satan left nothing to chance. His devious plan even had an inside man. Luke teaches, "Then Satan entered Judas, surnamed Iscariot, who was numbered among the twelve" (Luke 22:3). Satan would indwell Judas and use him to execute his climactic plan. This man, Judas Iscariot, would prove to be instrumental in handing the incarnate Son of God over to be crucified. Judas, "went his way and conferred with the chief priests and captains, how he might betray Him to them" (Luke 22:4).

It was Judas who led the enemies of Christ to Him, "And while He was still speaking, behold, a multitude; and he who was called Judas, one of the twelve, went before them and drew near to Jesus to kiss Him. But Jesus said to him, 'Judas, are you betraying the Son of Man with a kiss?'" (Luke 22:47-48). Jesus was arrested, mocked, and beaten (Luke 22:54, 63-64). The chief priests and the scribes made their false accusations (Luke 23:10). Even with a fraudulent trial, Jesus was found to be innocent of the charges against Him (Luke 23:14-15). The crowd would not listen, but instead they shouted, "Crucify Him, crucify Him!" (Luke 23:21). Within twenty-four hours Jesus had been arrested, tried, and condemned to die.

The light of men was extinguished. "Now it was about the sixth hour, and there was darkness over all the earth until the ninth hour. Then the sun was darkened, and the veil of the temple was torn in two. And when Jesus had cried out with a loud voice, He said, 'Father, "into Your hands I commit My spirit."' Having said this, He breathed His last" (Luke 23:44-46).

The body of the promised Messiah of Israel was placed into a tomb by Joseph of Arimathea. Joseph himself was a disciple of Jesus (John 19:38). Joseph, "was also waiting for the kingdom of God" (Luke 23:51). The immediate hope of the reign of the Messiah was postponed. It was the darkest hour in human history, and it seemed that Satan had won.

The rest of the story has been engraved into the pages of history. Lucifer had no cause for celebration because his perceived victory was actually God's redemptive sacrifice. Even men feared what the proclamation of His resurrection would mean. Matthew informs us:

On the next day, which followed the Day of Preparation, the chief priests and Pharisees gathered together to Pilate, saying, "Sir, we remember, while He was still alive, how that deceiver said, 'After three days I will rise.' Therefore command that the tomb be made secure until the third day, lest His disciples come by night and steal Him away, and say to the people, 'He has risen from the dead.' So the last deception will be worse than the first" (Matt. 27:62-64).

There was an element of truth in the words of the chief priests and Pharisees. The Lord Jesus had offered His resurrection as proof of His claim to be the Messiah. Matthew again instructs, "But He answered and said to them, 'An evil and adulterous generation seeks after a sign, and no sign will be given to it except the sign of the prophet Jonah. For as Jonah was three days and three nights in the belly of the great fish, so will the Son of Man be three days and three nights in the heart of the earth'" (Matt. 12:39-40). Jesus knew that He would be betrayed by the religious leaders of Israel, "and He began to teach them that the Son of Man must suffer many things, and be rejected by the elders and chief priests and scribes, and be killed, and after three days rise again" (Mark 8:31).

If Jesus was a counterfeit, He would not rise from the grave. With a powerful testimony the angel proclaimed to the women at the door of the tomb, "Do not be afraid, for I know that you seek Jesus who was crucified. He is not here; for He is risen, as He said. Come, see the place where the Lord lay. And go quickly and tell His disciples that He is risen from the dead, and indeed He is going before you into Galilee; there you will see Him. Behold, I have told you" (Matt. 28:5-7). Jesus had overcome death, hell, and the grave. Jesus proved Himself to be the Christ by rising from the grave.

Jesus had overcome death, hell, and the grave. Jesus proved Himself to be the Christ by rising from the grave.

Any celebration by Lucifer after the death of Christ was premature because Satan had been defeated by the resurrection of Jesus. Satan must have shrieked in horror as he realized he had been a pawn in the Father's plan. The great irony is that Satan's participation in the arrest and crucifixion of Jesus led to his own defeat. The writer of Hebrews mentions of Christ, "He Himself likewise shared in the same, that through death He might destroy him who had the power of death, that is, the devil" (Heb. 2:14). Satan has lost the power of death over the redeemed in Christ. Death is no longer something the believer in Christ must fear. The writer of Hebrews continues by testifying that Christ has released, "those who through fear of death were all their lifetime subject to bondage" (Heb. 2:15). What a glorious truth this is for the family of God!

Satan evidently underestimated the wisdom of God. The men that Satan used in his diabolical plan did not understand the purpose of Christ's crucifixion and the power of His resurrection. If they would have known God's purpose for the death of Christ, "they would not have crucified the Lord of glory" (1 Cor. 2:8). The death of Christ secured Satan's ultimate defeat.

Yet, like a dog guarding his bone, Satan refused to surrender. He reformulated his plan and determined to drag as many souls as possible to, "the everlasting fire prepared for the devil and his angels" (Matt. 25:41). Instead of waving the white flag of surrender, Satan dug in for battle.

For 2,000 more years Satan has sought to overcome good with evil. Scripture describes him as:

- the ruler of this world (John 12:31)
- the prince of the power of the air (Eph. 2:2)
- the god of this age (2 Cor. 4:4)
- the father of lies (John 8:44)

Satan will stop at nothing short of total world domination. During the Tribulation the Lord will allow Satan and his forces to rule every nation on earth (Rev. 13:3-8). The ruler of this world will establish a new world order, consistent with his character, which will rule all of mankind. It will be a kingdom founded on lies and built by deception.

When the Church Age comes to an end, Satan's plan is ready to be implemented at a moment's notice. It will involve yet another dark moment in human history.

Once again, Satan will leave nothing to chance. This time around the man that Satan likely will indwell is known to us in the Word of God as the *Antichrist*. Paul described the Antichrist as the man of sin and the son of perdition (2 Thess. 2:3). The Apostle John warned, "Little children, it is the last hour; and as you have heard that the Antichrist is coming, even now many antichrists have come, by which we know that it is the last hour" (1 John 2:18). Even as these words were first recorded, many antichrists had come. The antichrists that John referred to are deceptive and opposed to God, but their presence is one of the ways we know that we are living in the last days. There is one man whose opposition to God will stand above all the rest. The coming Antichrist will step onto the stage to rule the world.

Is the Antichrist Alive Today?

Satan has a man ready to come on the scene and oppose Christ.

A common question in eschatological discussions is, "Do you think the Antichrist is alive today?" The answer may surprise you. I do believe that at any time, in every generation, Satan has a man ready to come on the scene and oppose Christ. I suspect he might even have more than one. This man will be manipulating his way into an influential national position and awaiting his international opportunity.

It is imperative to remember that Satan is not in charge of the end times. Jesus Christ will return at the Father's appointed time (Matt. 24:36-44). Satan has no access to God's calendar. His plan is in place, but he has neither the power nor the authority to initiate the end time events. Satan cannot know when Jesus will return, and so therefore it is probable that Satan has a man ready in every generation. It is not unreasonable to believe that some of the men from history who attempted to conquer the world were the chosen candidates for their generations. Satan tried to establish his kingdom through them, but God crushed his attempts. We are left wondering if Napoleon, Lenin, and Hitler were the men Satan chose in their respective generations.

There is plenty about the Antichrist that we do know. The Antichrist will sweep into the political arena of the world when civilization is teetering on the brink of economic and political collapse. Multiple nations will be racing toward mutually-assured military annihilation. Nations will be desperate for an international leader, any leader, to come to the rescue.

The Antichrist will fill the leadership void. At first, he will accomplish what has seemed impossible. The Antichrist will negotiate peace in the Middle East (Dan. 9:27). He will promise to bring economic prosperity and order to a chaotic world. His deception will charm the nations. Billions of people throughout the world will gladly submit to his leadership and worship him. Even many within Israel will be deceived.

Deceived Again?

It almost seems unimaginable that this will happen. Given all of the unmistakable signs that are laid out in Scripture, how could the majority of the Jews fall into deception a second time? How is it that they will be persuaded to follow a false christ?

The answer to these questions rests with how the people of Israel responded to the First Advent of their Messiah. The signs of His First Coming were quite clear. The Hebrew prophets said the Messiah would be:

- born of a virgin (Isa. 7:14)
- born in Bethlehem (Micah 5:2)
- preceded by a forerunner who would herald His arrival (Mal. 3:1)
- demonstrating undeniable signs: the deaf would hear, the blind would see, lepers would be healed, the lame would walk, and the poor would have the good news preached to them (Isa. 35:5-6; 61:1)

The New Testament confirms the fulfillment of these prophecies at the First Coming of Jesus Christ. Jesus was:

- born of a virgin (Matt. 1:18-25; Luke 1:26-37)
- born in Bethlehem (Matt. 2:1; Luke 2:1-6)

- preceded by His forerunner and herald, John the Baptist (John 1:6-8, 15, 19-20)
- the One who healed the deaf, the blind, the lepers, and the lame while also preaching the gospel to the poor (Matt. 11:5)

The fulfillment of the signs predicted by the Hebrew prophets did not stop the majority of the Jewish people from rejecting Christ. He simply did not fit into the created mold of what they were looking for in a Messiah. They craved a political leader instead of a Savior.

A nation of people exclusively set apart for God missed the signs predicted by their own prophets. It is precisely for this reason we should not be surprised that this will happen a second time. Once again, people will long for a political leader instead of a Savior. Once again, the world will be distracted and blinded by geo-political world events. And yes, once again, many will miss what is hidden in plain sight.

The Current Battle

The written revelation of God helps us to recognize the enemy's current plan of attack. The god of this age has set out to blind the people of this world to the truth of the Gospel of Christ (2 Cor. 4:3-4). The overwhelming evidence around us confirms the teaching of Scripture that we are living in a time when, "the whole world lies under the sway of the wicked one" (1 John 5:19). The Scriptures also warn that we live in an age when Satan is the prince and, "evil men and impostors will grow worse and worse, deceiving and being deceived" (2 Tim. 3:13). This epic battle for truth is taking place because of the great last days deception that is now upon us. With our eyes wide open, we now set out on a course to fully comprehend the impact of the deception of our time.

This epic battle for truth is taking place because of the great last days deception that is now upon us.

Discussion Questions – Chapter 1

1. What was the darkest hour of human history?

2. How did Jesus win the victory over Satan?

3. How did Satan respond to his defeat?

4. Who is the Antichrist? What role will he play in Satan's plan?

5. How will most people respond to the Antichrist? Why?

Chapter 2

The Battle Intensifies

Beware lest anyone cheat you through philosophy and empty deceit, according to the tradition of men, according to the basic principles of the world, and not according to Christ. - Colossians 2:8

Germany, Italy, Japan, France, Great Britain, the United States, the Soviet Union, and China battled for the future of mankind.[1] It was the greatest war this world has ever seen. An estimated 40,000,000 – 50,000,000 people would ultimately lose their lives in this epic struggle against tyranny. The Second World War dominated the landscape of Europe.

By 1944, the Allied forces had wounded the German war machine. The invasion at Normandy gave the Allied troops a solid foothold in France. The liberation of France was rapid, but by September of 1944 the Allied forces were stalled on the border of Germany. This is when the German army proved that the war was not over yet.

History has demonstrated convincingly that these were the last days of the war on the European front, but Germany had one last major offensive left. It has become known to students of history as the Battle of the Bulge. The primary goal for Germany was to retake the Port of Antwerp. Fortunately, instead of breaking the Allied lines, the German forces were only capable of creating a bulge. This last ditch effort used far more resources than Germany could afford. It was a desperate attempt at victory that ended up costing Germany 220,000 soldiers and contributed to their final defeat the following spring.

Let it be recognized that another powerful battle is currently raging for the control of this earth. It is a fierce spiritual battle, and all corners of the earth are bulging from its repercussions. The Word of God describes the time we are living in as the *last days* or the *last hour*. This long fought battle will soon be coming to an end. Satan is exhausting every effort in his attempt to achieve victory. The closer we get to the end of the battle the more the lies and deception will increase, underscoring the importance of being alert to the conflict that besets us. Satan's final push before the inauguration of Christ's Kingdom will come during the Tribulation when the Antichrist takes control of the world.

> *The Word of God describes the time we are living in as the last days or the last hour.*

What are the Last Days?

The *last days* is a biblical expression that is often misunderstood. It is closely related to the Church Age. Students of the Bible should recognize that the Church Age was not explicitly revealed in the Old Testament. The New Testament confirmed this truth about the Church when Paul proclaimed, "which in other ages was not made known to the sons of men" (Eph. 3:5). The Church Age began with the birth of the Church on the day of Pentecost (Acts 2:1). This age of grace will come to an end with the removal of the Church at the Rapture (1 Thess. 1:10).

The *last days* are a little more difficult to define. It is tempting to see the expression *last days*, or similar statements, and assume that they are always referring to the same period of time. Truthfully, each section of Scripture must be examined closely in its context to determine the specific meaning intended.

To illustrate, consider a passage from Deuteronomy 4:

> But from there you will seek the LORD your God, and you will find Him if you seek Him with all your heart and with all your soul. When you are in distress, and all these things come upon you in the latter days, when you turn to the LORD

your God and obey His voice (for the LORD your God is a merciful God), He will not forsake you nor destroy you, nor forget the covenant of your fathers which He swore to them (Deut. 4:29-31).

In this Old Testament example the *latter days* is the focus of our attention. The original audience was the physical descendants of Abraham, Isaac, and Jacob. The meaning of *latter days* is simply a reference to future days.[2] However, we must ask the question if there has ever been a time when the people of Israel turned to the Lord in *complete* obedience? The obvious answer is that there has never been an occasion when this has been historically fulfilled. Therefore, this prophecy awaits a future fulfillment. The context points to a future when the people of Israel will be scattered abroad in distress. The Hebrew people were told that they would then, "turn to the LORD your God and obey His voice" (Deut. 4:30).

The Tribulation will be a brutal period for the people of Israel. It will be a time when Satan persecutes the nation of Israel. The Word of God teaches that two-thirds of the Jewish people will be killed (Zech. 13:8-9). More than any other moment in history, the Hebrew people will need to be reminded, "(for the LORD your God is a merciful God), He will not forsake you nor destroy you, nor forget the covenant of your fathers which He swore to them" (Deut. 4:31). This prophecy from Deuteronomy will be fulfilled at the end of the Tribulation when the Lord Jesus Christ returns to fulfill His covenant promises and establish His Kingdom on earth.

The point of this exercise is to recognize that in this Old Testament example the phrase *latter days* indicates the end of the Tribulation. Other Old Testament passages use similar expressions in different ways. In both Isaiah 2:2-4 and Micah 4:1-7 the *latter days* refer to the Kingdom of Christ on earth. Context always determines the meaning.

The Last Days in the New Testament

As we approach the New Testament we immediately recognize the primary audience shifts from the nation of Israel to the Church.

Yet, even within the New Testament there is some variation in both the terminology and the context in which these expressions are used.

The Apostle Peter testified of Christ, "He indeed was foreordained before the foundation of the world, but was manifest in these last times for you" (1 Pet. 1:20). This particular usage of the *last days* refers to the period of time that starts with the manifestation of Christ to men.

The opening words of the book of Hebrews highlight the historical shift to the last days. The writer stated, "God, who at various times and in various ways spoke in time past to the fathers by the prophets, has in these last days spoken to us by His Son" (Heb. 1:1-2). A remarkable contrast is made within these two verses between the expressions *in time past* and *these last days*. An indicator of the last days is the revelation of God through His Son Jesus Christ.[3]

The Lord Jesus Christ made this same type of contrast in His own ministry when He said, "For all the prophets and the law prophesied until John" (Matt. 11:13). Central to this discussion is the fact that, "John the Baptist was the last of the Old Testament prophets. His ministry terminated the revelatory age of the past, although the written expression of divine revelation ended with the Book of Malachi."[4]

God's ultimate communication is through Jesus Christ. The New Testament faithfully reveals Him. This foundational truth desperately needs to be understood in this age. Arnold Fruchtenbaum teaches:

> The prophets often spoke of the Messianic Age as "in the last days." It is now the messianic times because the Messiah has come, and He was the focal point toward whom all this previous revelation was pointing. The Apostles, of course, wrote the New Testament after Jesus left, but the content of what they wrote had to do with His life, His ministry, His words, and His teachings. What they wrote had to do with the significance of His coming.[5]

Nestled into the first epistle from the Apostle John we find a similar expression, "Little children, it is the last hour; and as you have heard that the Antichrist is coming, even now many antichrists have come, by which we know that it is the last hour" (1 John 2:18). The false teachers present in John's day indicated that the last hour was upon the Church. This was not intended to signify a specific time, but rather, "the beginning of the end of all things."[6]

The Last Days and the Church Age

Within the New Testament, especially in Pauline literature, the last days has a particular focus on the present Church Age. Paul warned Timothy about what would come during this time:

> Now the Spirit expressly says that in latter times some will depart from the faith, giving heed to deceiving spirits and doctrines of demons, speaking lies in hypocrisy, having their own conscience seared with a hot iron, forbidding to marry, and commanding to abstain from foods which God created to be received with thanksgiving by those who believe and know the truth (1 Tim. 4:1-3).

In this instance Paul used slightly different terminology and referred to *latter times*. Paul wanted Timothy to know that there would be times when believers in Christ will fail to hold to the doctrines of their faith. The Apostle was not suggesting believers can lose their salvation (Eph. 4:30). This is a simple admonition from Paul that there would be times coming when believers paid more attention to the doctrines of demons than the doctrines of faith in Jesus Christ. There is nothing within the context of this passage to suggest that Paul was referring to unbelievers masking themselves as believers and then departing the faith. Instead, "'the faith' here denotes the doctrinal truths of the Christian faith. ... An apostate is not one who gives up his profession of being a Christian, but one who forsakes the truth of the Christian faith."[7] It is self-evident from Scripture that believers can walk in disobedience to the Lord, which impacts their ability to hold to the doctrines of Christ (1 Cor. 3:1-3).

Again, Timothy was told, "But know this, that in the last days perilous times will come" (2 Tim. 3:1). On this occasion Paul used the expression *last days* to describe the hard times that would come. Timothy was forewarned that:

 Men will be lovers of themselves, lovers of money, boasters, proud, blasphemers, disobedient to parents, unthankful, unholy, unloving, unforgiving, slanderers, without self-control, brutal, despisers of good, traitors, headstrong, haughty, lovers of pleasure rather than lovers of God, having a form of godliness but denying its power. And from such people turn away! For of this sort are those who creep into households and make captives of gullible women loaded down with sins, led away by various lusts, always learning and never able to come to the knowledge of the truth (2 Tim. 3:2-7).

A better description of the Church Age could not be written. The undeniable witness of Scripture is the continued pattern of disobedience to the Lord.

The Apostle Peter's teaching about the last days is remarkably consistent with Paul's. Peter writes, "knowing this first: that scoffers will come in the last days, walking according to their own lusts, and saying, 'Where is the promise of His coming? For since the fathers fell asleep, all things continue as they were from the beginning of creation'" (2 Pet. 3:3-4). It is a sign of the times that scoffers mock the coming of the Lord Jesus Christ during the Church Age.

An interpretive question arises at this point. Consider the key terminology of these last three passages:

- in latter times some will depart from the faith (1 Tim. 4:1)
- in the last days perilous times will come (2 Tim. 3:1)
- scoffers will come in the last days (2 Pet. 3:3)

A casual reading of these texts can give rise to a misinterpretation of Scripture. The apostles were not suggesting that at the *end* of the Church Age there will be a rampant moral decline. Rather, they were teaching that spiritual apostasy will characterize the *entire* Church Age and increase in intensity.

In 2 Timothy 3:5 Paul instructed Timothy to turn away from the disobedient men of his day. Paul already considered this form of contempt for God present in Ephesus. He was warning that during these last days, which span the entire Church Age, there would be times when this type of rebellion against the Lord would exist.

Even though Paul was not predicting a moral decline towards the end of the Church Age, he did tell Timothy, "But evil men and impostors will grow worse and worse, deceiving and being deceived" (2 Tim. 3:13). This key truth provides the underlying premise for this present book. It stands as a constant reminder to the Church that as time progresses the deception will continue to increase. It will become easier and easier to be deceived. And it will become easier and easier to deceive. The lies of the imposters will feed on themselves. As more men are led into deception, the cycle will continue to grow worse as we move deeper into these last days.

As more men are led into deception, the cycle will continue to grow worse as we move deeper into these last days.

The Battle of the Last Days

The unsettling reality of the last days was predicted in the New Testament. Early on in the progress of the revelation of the New Testament the Apostle Paul referred to this time as, "this present evil age" (Gal. 1:4). Paul instructed the church at Corinth that, "the god of this age has blinded" unbelievers to Christ's glorious light of the gospel (2 Cor. 4:4).

The Apostle Paul felt it was necessary to warn the church at Ephesus about the certainty of the battle we face, "For we do not wrestle against flesh and blood, but against principalities, against powers, against the rulers of the darkness of this age, against spiritual hosts of wickedness in the heavenly places" (Eph. 6:12). The satanic influences in this world will lead to great deception.

The satanic influences in this world will lead to great deception.

The front lines of this battle are all around us. The Devil, "walks about like a roaring lion, seeking whom he may devour" (1 Pet. 5:8). We are to, "Resist him, steadfast in the faith, knowing that the same sufferings are experienced by your brotherhood in the world" (1 Pet. 5:9).

Without the Commander of the army of the Lord physically present during the Church Age we are instructed to, "walk by faith, not by sight" (Josh. 5:14-15; Rev. 19:19; 2 Cor. 5:7). Living with this trust in Jesus Christ will enable believers to deny, "ungodliness and worldly lusts," and, "live soberly, righteously, and godly in the present age" (Titus 2:12). Paul laid out our battle plan:

Finally, my brethren, be strong in the Lord and in the power of His might. Put on the whole armor of God, that you may be able to stand against the wiles of the devil. For we do not wrestle against flesh and blood, but against principalities, against powers, against the rulers of the darkness of this age, against spiritual hosts of wickedness in the heavenly places. Therefore take up the whole armor of God, that you may be able to withstand in the evil day, and having done all, to stand. Stand therefore, having girded your waist with truth, having put on the breastplate of righteousness, and having shod your feet with the preparation of the gospel of peace; above all, taking the shield of faith with which you will be able to quench all the fiery darts of the wicked one. And take the helmet of salvation, and the sword of the Spirit, which is the word of God (Eph. 6:10-17).

The battle for truth will rapidly intensify in these last days. Great comfort should come from knowing that God has equipped His people with the resources required to stand against the relentless forces of deception. With profound wisdom Paul admonished the believers at Ephesus, "See then that you walk circumspectly, not as fools but as wise, redeeming the time, because the days are evil" (Eph. 5:15-16). May it be that we live for Christ during these last days with our confident hope in the glorious return of our Savior!

Discussion Questions – Chapter 2

1. Is there a difference between the last days and the Church Age?

2. What is the revelation of God through Jesus Christ an indicator of?

3. As the Church Age progresses, what will continue to increase?

4. When will the last days for the Church come to an end?

5. As Church Age believers, what should we be doing in these final days?

Endnotes - Chapter 2

1. These were the primary leaders of the Allied and Axis powers during WWII.

2. Ludwig Koehler, Walter Baumgartner, M.E.J Richardson, and Johann Jakob Stamm, *The Hebrew and Aramaic Lexicon of the Old Testament* (Leiden, New York: E.J. Brill, 1999), 36.

3. Homer Kent reminds us, "A literal rendering of the Greek time expression here translated in these last days would be 'at the last of these days,' and it is tempting to interpret it as meaning 'recently.' Thus the author would be calling attention to the recent occurrence of the revelation in Christ, coming at the end of the Old Testament period previously mentioned. However, it must be recognized that this is precisely the Septuagint rendering of the frequent Old Testament expression *be' aherith hayyāmim* ('in the end of the days'), which usually denoted messianic times in some way (see Num. 24:14, et al.). Hence the author should be understood to say that the last days have been inaugurated with the coming of Messiah. ... In these momentous times God has spoken in a Son." Homer Kent, Jr., *The Epistle to the Hebrews: A Commentary* (Winona Lake, IN: BMH Books, 2002), 35-36.

4. Robert Gromacki, Dr., *Stand Bold in Grace: An Exposition of Hebrews* (The Woodlands, TX: Kress Christian Publications, 2002), 23.

5. Arnold G. Fruchtenbaum, *The Messianic Jewish Epistles: Hebrews, James, First Peter, Second Peter, Jude*, 1st ed. (Tustin, CA: Ariel Ministries, 2005), 18-19.

6. Earl D. Radmacher, Ronald Barclay Allen, and H. Wayne House, *Nelson's New Illustrated Bible Commentary* (Nashville, TN: T. Nelson Publishers, 1999), 1 John 2:18.

7. D. Edmond Hiebert, *Everyman's Bible Commentary: First Timothy* (Chicago, IL: Moody Press, 1957), 76.

Chapter 3

The Times and the Seasons

But concerning the times and the seasons, brethren, you have no need that I should write to you. For you yourselves know perfectly that the day of the Lord so comes as a thief in the night. For when they say, "Peace and safety!" then sudden destruction comes upon them, as labor pains upon a pregnant woman. And they shall not escape. But you, brethren, are not in darkness, so that this Day should overtake you as a thief. You are all sons of light and sons of the day. We are not of the night nor of darkness. Therefore let us not sleep, as others do, but let us watch and be sober. - 1 Thessalonians 5:1-6

Insignificant events tend to be the forces that shape the world. The 1970 election of Salvador Allende Gossens to the presidency of Chile framed the political landscape of Chile that would define the nation for decades.

Those who do not know the past are doomed to repeat it.

The maxim is true: *Those who do not know the past are doomed to repeat it.* To put it another way, the past can often be a guide to what the future may bring. Allende's past was rooted in the radical politics of Marxism, which resulted in strong opposition to him in the 1970 presidential election. In a three-way race, Allende could only muster up 36.3 percent of the vote, but it was enough to overcome the opposition. Under the leadership of

President Nixon, the United States strategically attempted to keep Allende from coming to power, but this effort failed.

The destructive policies that Allende embraced led to an uproar. United States copper companies were taken over by the Chilean government and no compensation was given. Large estates were broken up so the land could be worked by the poor farmers. The desire to have economic equality led to wage increases and price freezes. In an effort to pay off the large debt Allende had created, more currency was minted. Inflation, food shortages, and strikes helped to fuel civil unrest.

Allende had many enemies, both foreign and domestic. At the front of the foreign opposition was the government of the United States. Efforts were focused on assisting the overthrow of Allende by secretly aiding the Chilean opposition and applying economic pressure. The Central Intelligence Agency of the United States covertly sent at least ten million dollars to groups that stood in opposition to Allende in order to undermine his regime. The economic pressure that was put into place by the United States was stifling. Funds were blocked from the International Monetary Fund, the World Bank, and the Inter-American Development Bank. The strong hand of the government of the United States was persuasive in keeping countries from investing in Chile, which intensified the pressure on Allende.

September 11, 1973 was a day most Chileans will never forget. On that day, Allende was ousted from power by a vicious military coup led by General Augusto Pinochet Ugarte. The presidential palace was surrounded by army troops and bombarded with rocket fire. Allende was found dead from the bullets that had torn through his body.

The conflict had been won by the right. The leftist Marxists had clearly lost the battle of control for the nation of Chile. Did this mean freedom would now reign?

Instead of freedom, the military ruled the country with General Pinochet at the helm. The Constitution was suspended, Congress was dissolved, censorship was put into place, and all political parties were forced to disband. The military launched a campaign to eliminate the leftist element from the Chilean society. Many thousands of people were arrested and tortured. Scores were executed, while yet others simply disappeared. Chile remained a police state until March of 1990.[1]

The turmoil in Chile came in two stages because it was two separate authoritarians who caused the upheaval. Allende abused the power that was legitimately entrusted to him to enforce his leftist policies. The brutal dictatorship of Pinochet cost the lives of thousands of Chileans. Both sides of the political spectrum stood guilty of leaving a permanent scar on the landscape of liberty. It was a dangerous time to live in Chile, but the reign of each man was quite distinct from the other.

A Look at the Differences

Within the unfolding plan of God, the troubling times of this world also will go through separate stages. Each period of time has its own challenges, but it is essential to recognize the great differences between the last days and the end times.

> *The Rapture is a pivotal moment that also signals the end of the Church Age.*

As we have already witnessed, the last days for the Church is the time between the day of Pentecost and the Rapture. The Rapture of the Church is the event that begins the end times and it continues through the establishment of the eternal Messianic Kingdom (Rev. 21:1). The Rapture is a pivotal moment that also signals the end of the Church Age.

During the Church Age we can take great comfort from knowing that all who are saved by grace through faith in Jesus Christ go directly to heaven when they die. The Apostle Paul boldly stated, "We are confident, yes, well pleased rather to be absent from the body and to be present with the Lord" (2 Cor. 5:8). Even before the Church Age began, when believers died they went to be with the Lord. Jesus promised to the criminal on the cross, "Assuredly, I say to you, today you will be with Me in Paradise" (Luke 23:43).

The Rapture of the Church directly impacts every believer in Christ from the Church Age. The return of Christ for His Church will be a global event. First, Jesus Christ will bring the Church Age saints who have already died with Him. Paul said, "For if we believe that Jesus died and rose again, even so God will bring with Him those who sleep in Jesus" (1 Thess. 4:14). It is at that time that the dead in Christ will receive their new glorified bodies. This is confirmed by the words of Paul when he testified, "And the dead in Christ will rise first" (1 Thess. 4:16).

Immediately after this, believers in Christ who are alive on the earth will be caught up (raptured) and will instantly be with the Lord Jesus. Paul again taught, "Then we who are alive and remain shall be caught up together with them in the clouds to meet the Lord in the air" (1 Thess. 4:17).

At that moment our bodies will be transformed. Referring to believers receiving these new glorified bodies Paul told the church at Corinth, "the dead will be raised incorruptible, and we shall be changed. For this corruptible must put on incorruption, and this mortal must put on immortality" (1 Cor. 15:52-53). This transformation will take place, "in a moment, in the twinkling of an eye" (1 Cor. 15:52).

Tucked into Paul's instruction about the Rapture, to the church at Thessalonica, we find an exceptional promise. There we read, "And thus we shall always be with the Lord" (1 Thess. 4:17). The Church will return to heaven with Christ while the Tribulation on earth rages. This is our, "blessed hope" (Titus 2:13).

Take a look at figure 3.1. The small circle at the lower left indicates the Church Age, which is what Paul referred to as the last days (2 Tim. 3:1). This is where we are on God's prophetic calendar right now. The larger circle calls attention to the end times, which begins with the Rapture of the Church.

Figure 3.1

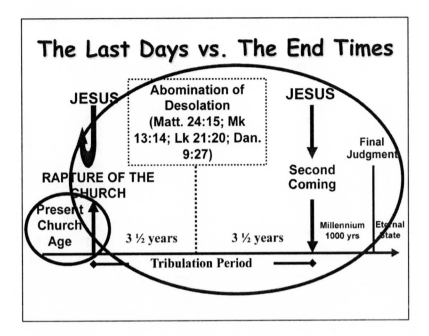

The Last Days vs. The End Times

JESUS

Abomination of Desolation (Matt. 24:15; Mk 13:14; Lk 21:20; Dan. 9:27)

JESUS

Final Judgment

RAPTURE OF THE CHURCH

Second Coming

Present Church Age

3 ½ years

3 ½ years

Millennium 1000 yrs

Eternal State

Tribulation Period

The Rapture will open the door for Satan to inaugurate his end times plan.

The Rapture will open the door for Satan to inaugurate his end times plan. After the Rapture, the end time events on earth will begin to unfold quickly. The seven-year Tribulation period, also known as Daniel's Seventieth Week, will begin.

Scripture describes this future seven-year slice of history in foreboding terms. It will be the "great day of His [God's] wrath" (Rev. 6:17).

This period of time will be so severe that people struggling to survive will cry out in despair, "Who is able to stand?" (Rev. 6:17). It is easy to see why the prophets labeled this coming time as:

- a day of darkness and gloom (Zeph. 1:15; Amos 5:18, 20; Joel 2:2)

- a day of calamity and distress (Deut. 32:35; Obad. 12-14)
- the overflowing scourge (Isa. 28:15, 18)
- the time of Jacob's trouble (Jer. 30:7)

Halfway through the Tribulation is a transitional event. Jesus spoke of it as, "The 'abomination of desolation,' spoken of by Daniel the prophet" (Matt. 24:15; Mark 13:14; Luke 21:20; Dan. 9:27). This is the event that begins the second half of the Tribulation, often referred to as the Great Tribulation. Speaking of this time Jesus said, "For then there will be great tribulation, such as has not been since the beginning of the world until this time, no, nor ever shall be" (Matt. 24:21).

> *The abomination of desolation is a pivotal moment when the Antichrist will declare his own deity.*

The abomination of desolation is a pivotal moment when the Antichrist will declare his own deity. The newly rebuilt temple in Jerusalem will be transformed into a place where the citizens of the world will be required to worship him. Paul instructed, "Let no one deceive you by any means; for that Day will not come unless the falling away comes first, and the man of sin is revealed, the son of perdition, who opposes and exalts himself above all that is called God or that is worshiped, so that he sits as God in the temple of God, showing himself that he is God" (2 Thess. 2:3-4).

The Tribulation will end with the Second Coming of Jesus to earth. The Lord Jesus will crush Satan's forces at the Battle of Armageddon and will establish His reign on earth during the Millennium. Revelation teaches:

> Now I saw heaven opened, and behold, a white horse. And He who sat on him was called Faithful and True, and in righteousness He judges and makes war. ... And the armies in heaven, clothed in fine linen, white and clean, followed Him on white horses. Now out of His mouth goes a sharp sword, that with it He should strike the nations. ... And I saw

the beast, the kings of the earth, and their armies, gathered together to make war against Him who sat on the horse and against His army. Then the beast was captured, and with him the false prophet who worked signs in his presence, by which he deceived those who received the mark of the beast and those who worshiped his image. These two were cast alive into the lake of fire burning with brimstone. And the rest were killed with the sword which proceeded from the mouth of Him who sat on the horse (Rev. 19:11, 14-15, 19-21).

A Look Ahead

The Tribulation will be a time when the end times intersect directly with the lies of Satan. Daniel's future Seventieth Week will be the height of the spiritual battle. The deception during this time will be fierce. Paul warned, "The coming of the lawless one is according to the working of Satan, with all power, signs, and lying wonders, and with all unrighteous deception among those who perish, because they did not receive the love of the truth, that they might be saved" (2 Thess. 2:9-10). The revelation of God given to Daniel is the key to understanding the confrontation ahead. We turn our attention there next.

Discussion Questions – Chapter 3

1. When are the end times?

2. How does Scripture describe the Tribulation Period? How long will it last?

3. Where will the Church be during the Tribulation?

4. How and when will the Tribulation end?

5. Describe the key differences between the last days and the end times.

Endnotes - Chapter 3

1. For a sobering reflection on the political turmoil of Chile in 1973, see http://www.santiagotimes.cl/chile/human-rights-a-law/23240-chilean-police-testimonies-reveal-horrific-details-on-1973-coup.

Chapter 4

Israel and God's Prophetic Road Map

Brethren, my heart's desire and prayer to God for Israel is
that they may be saved. ... I say then, has God cast away His
people? Certainly not! For I also am an Israelite, of the seed
of Abraham, of the tribe of Benjamin. God has not cast away
His people whom He foreknew. - Romans 10:1; 11:1-2

J acob seemed to defy the years of his age. Over eighty years of life
had not slowed him down. Still, the time had come to put words
down on paper describing the incredible events of his past. His
story started with the explanation of where he had come from.

Jacob was only a young boy when his parents had fled Europe.
He knew this part about his family history, but he needed some help
with the details. Up in the rafters of the attic Jacob would find the
answers he was looking for. Long ago his parents had kept some
souvenirs from their earlier years.

His mother was a strong, quiet woman. She talked very little
about her own family. Now that she had been gone for many years, it
left Jacob wishing he would have asked her more about the events of
her life. As Jacob climbed the old wooden stairs to the attic, he had
many more questions than answers.

A dusty old shoebox contained the story of his mother, Anichka.
She had been born near a small village in Ukraine, but left at a young
age to stay with her aunt in Poland. It was this single providential
event that spared her from certain death.

1932 marked the beginning of the Ukraine famine. It was a time when the Soviet Union, headed by Joseph Stalin, sought to take total control of the Ukrainian people by denying them the food they needed to survive. Independent farmers were seen as a threat to the state. The Soviet Union wanted the people to take up collective farming. The government took the farmers' homes, livestock, crops, and anything of substantial value. Heavy grain taxes forced the people into deliberate starvation. Resisting meant being shot to death or deported to Siberia. The wheat taken from the people was sold in foreign markets to fund Stalin's plan for transforming the Soviet Union. Extreme starvation set in and people even turned to cannibalism. An estimated 25,000 people were dying every day during the famine. Untold millions of people died from both starvation and execution.

Anichka had come from a family farm in Ukraine. Her brothers, sisters, mother, and father had all been forced into starvation. Jacob became painfully aware of how fortunate his own mother had been to escape the horrors of the Soviet Union.

To think of the atrocities his people suffered caused Jacob great heartache. His mind drifted forward to the rest of his family history. These types of brutal crimes against humanity had struck again. Jacob could actually remember the frantic discussions within his family about the Nazi Army advancing towards their village in Poland. The question burned in his mind of whether or not his extended family had escaped the German death machine. He turned his attention to the next box in the room.

The second dusty box contained relics from his father's life. It did not take long before he discovered the awful truth. A brittle old letter from a friend of the family revealed the tragic news. His uncle's family had died in the gas chambers of Auschwitz. Jacob knew that he was not alone in his anguish. Millions of Jewish people had been killed at the extermination camps. His family had been one of the fortunate few to escape. Still, the thoughts of the death and suffering of his people simmered within him.

How many times must the Jewish people suffer? Thousands of years of history seemed to imply that God had forsaken them. The

Hebrew people had continued to fail to turn to the Lord. Centuries of death had taken its toll on them. As a Messianic Jew, Jacob longed for the day when the promise of the Torah would come true:

> Then the LORD your God will bring you to the land which your fathers possessed, and you shall possess it. He will prosper you and multiply you more than your fathers. And the LORD your God will circumcise your heart and the heart of your descendants, to love the LORD your God with all your heart and with all your soul, that you may live (Deut. 30:5–6).

The Story of Daniel

Jacob was certainly not the first Jewish man to wonder about the suffering of his people. This is the true account of a man who lived long ago, by the name of Daniel.

The record of Daniel starts in the midst of some desperate days for the people of Israel. The northern kingdom of Israel had long been defeated by the Assyrians. Now it was time for the southern kingdom, Judah, to fall at the hands of the Babylonians. We are told:

> In the third year of the reign of Jehoiakim king of Judah, Nebuchadnezzar king of Babylon came to Jerusalem and besieged it. And the Lord gave Jehoiakim king of Judah into his hand, with some of the articles of the house of God, which he carried into the land of Shinar to the house of his god; and he brought the articles into the treasure house of his god (Dan. 1:1-2).

It is easy to pass over this introduction to Daniel without thinking of the significance of what had actually taken place. God's people had been defeated and His Temple was looted. For the Hebrew people this must have shaken the very foundation of their faith.

The written Word of God provides a lot of information about Daniel. He was a part of the select group of captives carried from Jerusalem to Babylon in 605 B.C. The record teaches:

> Then the king instructed Ashpenaz, the master of his eunuchs, to bring some of the children of Israel and some of the king's descendants and some of the nobles, young men in whom there was no blemish, but good-looking, gifted in all wisdom, possessing knowledge and quick to understand, who had ability to serve in the king's palace, and whom they might teach the language and literature of the Chaldeans (Dan. 1:3-4).

Daniel was selected as part of this group of young men (Dan. 1:6-7). He was probably, "about fourteen or fifteen years of age when he was taken into captivity and began his training."[1]

It is hard to imagine the great pressure that Daniel faced from his captors, but the evidence shows that Daniel refused to compromise his faith. He would remain loyal to the one true and living God. Even in these dire circumstances Daniel was able to distinguish himself amongst the captives chosen for training by the government (Dan. 1:1-19; 6:3).

While living in a foreign land Daniel was sustained by his faith. His habit for many years was to read God's Word and pray three times a day (Dan. 6:10). This man of God served the king of Babylon but continued to pray for his people and their homeland.

A Time to Remember

By the time we reach the ninth chapter of Daniel quite a bit of time has passed in Daniel's life. This young boy had grown into an old man who was now a high ranking government official still living in captivity. The evidence shows, "If taken captive about age fifteen in 605 B.C., he would have been over eighty years of age in 538 B.C."[2] Decades of living in a foreign land had not broken him down. His eyes were still fixed firmly upon God's Word.

Daniel had been studying the words of the prophet Jeremiah:

> In the first year of Darius the son of Ahasuerus, of the lineage of the Medes, who was made king over the realm of the Chaldeans— in the first year of his reign I, Daniel, understood by the books the number of the years specified by the word of the LORD through Jeremiah the prophet, that He would accomplish seventy years in the desolations of Jerusalem (Dan. 9:1-2).

A survey of Jeremiah reveals to us the Scripture that Daniel must have been reading. Two passages stand out above the rest:

> And this whole land shall be a desolation and an astonishment, and these nations shall serve the king of Babylon seventy years. "Then it will come to pass, when seventy years are completed, that I will punish the king of Babylon and that nation, the land of the Chaldeans, for their iniquity," says the LORD; "and I will make it a perpetual desolation" (Jer. 25:11-12).

> For thus says the LORD: After seventy years are completed at Babylon, I will visit you and perform My good word toward you, and cause you to return to this place. For I know the thoughts that I think toward you, says the LORD, thoughts of peace and not of evil, to give you a future and a hope (Jer. 29:10-11).

These words must have leaped out at Daniel. The God of Israel had promised to rescue His people from captivity. God had promised to return His people to their homeland after seventy years!

In order to fully grasp the excitement of the day we need to focus on the timeline involved. Daniel had been taken captive in 605 B.C. The year was now 538 B.C. This meant that Daniel had been in Babylon for sixty-seven years. God's promised restoration would be soon.

Even in his old age, Daniel longed to see Israel restored. Daniel wanted to see his people return to their homeland to rebuild

Jerusalem and the Temple. This desire still burned within him. The continued instruction found in Jeremiah gave Daniel his marching orders, "And you will seek Me and find Me, when you search for Me with all your heart. I will be found by you, says the LORD, and I will bring you back from your captivity" (Jer. 29:13-14). The inspiring record demonstrates this is exactly what he did, "Then I set my face toward the Lord God to make request by prayer and supplications, with fasting, sackcloth, and ashes" (Dan. 9:3).

Daniel devoted himself to prayer on behalf of the people of Israel. They stood guilty of failing to live in obedience to their God. Daniel acknowledged their sin and God's right to judge them. They had broken His Law and ignored His prophets. Their unfaithfulness to God led Daniel to plead for mercy:

> O my God, incline Your ear and hear; open Your eyes and see our desolations, and the city which is called by Your name; for we do not present our supplications before You because of our righteous deeds, but because of Your great mercies. O Lord, hear! O Lord, forgive! O Lord, listen and act! Do not delay for Your own sake, my God, for Your city and Your people are called by Your name (Dan. 9:18-19).

A Time to Listen

The response by God to Daniel's prayer would define the ages to come. The angel, Gabriel, was sent to reveal God's plan for both the people of Israel and Jerusalem. Consider part of the instruction given to Daniel, "Seventy weeks are determined for your people and for your holy city" (Dan. 9:24). This brief statement is packed with information that will affect the entire world. Essentially, God was revealing a specific 490-year plan for the nation of Israel and the world as a whole. This revelation was focused particularly on the Jewish people, with the holy city standing as a distinct reference to Jerusalem.

Of great interest is the particular phrase *seventy weeks*. Today people tend to think in decades, but we must remember that for the

Jewish people it was quite natural for them to think in terms of sevens. The literal wording in verse 24 is *seventy sevens*. In this case the usage of the word *weeks* is representative. Each day represents a year on the prophetic calendar, which would have been the natural understanding for Daniel. Therefore, 70 weeks are equal to 490 years. These are not to be understood as years according to our calendar. A prophetic year in the Bible is 360 days long.

> God will do everything necessary for the reconciliation, eternal salvation, and righteousness of His people.

This period of 490 years has a purpose. God will work, "to finish the transgression, to make an end of sins, to make reconciliation for iniquity, to bring in everlasting righteousness, to seal up vision and prophecy, and to anoint the Most Holy" (Dan. 9:24). God will do everything necessary for the reconciliation, eternal salvation, and righteousness of His people.

Notice the time markers in Daniel 9:25, "Know therefore and understand, that from the going forth of the command to restore and build Jerusalem until Messiah the Prince, there shall be seven weeks and sixty-two weeks; the street shall be built again, and the wall, even in troublesome times." The command to restore and rebuild Jerusalem came from the Persian ruler Artexerxes I, in March of 444 B.C. (Neh. 2:1-8).

From the time of this command in 444 B.C. Daniel was told that 69 weeks (483 years) would pass before the Messiah would come. The sixty-nine weeks is comprised of the seven weeks and sixty-two weeks, according to Daniel 9:25. Based on a 360 day prophetic year this works out to 173,880 days.

This prophecy in Daniel is without a doubt the key to understanding God's entire prophetic plan for the ages. This prophecy is so specific and accurate that it has led liberal scholars and skeptics to deny the authorship and/or date of this book of the Bible. Consider figure 4.1. Beginning with the historical decree of Artexerxes I on March 5, 444 B.C. and moving forward in time 173,880 days (as

Daniel's prophecy indicates), we arrive precisely at the time of Christ's triumphal entry! Moreover, following the end of this sixty-ninth week (483 years), Daniel's prophecy indicates that there will be a gap of time prior to the start of the seventieth week, during which at least two events will occur.

Figure 4.1

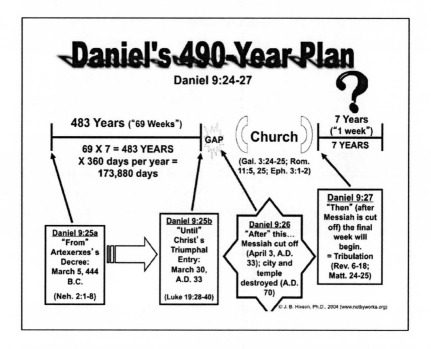

The events prophesied to occur during the gap between the sixty-ninth and seventieth weeks of Daniel are laid out for us in Scripture. This time the verse that grabs our attention is Daniel 9:26, "And after the sixty-two weeks Messiah shall be cut off, but not for Himself; and the people of the prince who is to come shall destroy the city and the sanctuary. The end of it shall be with a flood, and till the end of the war desolations are determined." Since we picked up Daniel 9:26 in midstream, it should be remembered that the sixty-two weeks are a part of the first sixty-nine weeks in God's plan for Israel. After this time the Messiah would be cut off, indicating that He would be killed. Notice that Daniel was told the Messiah's death would be, "not for Himself" (Dan. 9:26). Here we have a strong prophecy of the vicarious death of the Messiah, which came to be in A.D. 33 (Luke 23:44-47; 1 Cor. 15:3).

There is a great distinction in Daniel 9:25-26 between the Messiah the Prince and the prince who is to come. The latter is a reference to the coming Antichrist. Verse 26 of Daniel teaches that his people would destroy the city of Jerusalem and its Temple. Here is where paying attention to the details, the context, and the wording used in Scripture helps us to understand the original intent of the text.

We remember that the latter part of verse 26 is referring to the time following the crucifixion of the Messiah. This places us in the first century after the death of the Savior. Surely the Antichrist was not ruling at that time, but the Roman Empire was. One day the Antichrist will rule the final or revived Roman Empire (Dan. 7:8). Therefore, the people of the Antichrist who would destroy the city of Jerusalem and the Temple were the people of the Roman Empire. This is exactly what happened when the Roman army destroyed Jerusalem and the Temple in A.D. 70. "The end of it shall be with a flood, and till the end of the war desolations are determined" (Dan. 9:26). The destruction of Jerusalem would be like the devastation caused in an overwhelming flood.

> *The destruction of Jerusalem would be like the devastation caused in an overwhelming flood.*

It would be easy to miss the significance of how verse 27 of Daniel 9 begins. The word *then* is a marker of time. It signifies that what is being described in verse 27 must follow the events of verse 26. So now we need to work our way through the progression outlined in the passage.

- Verse 25 describes a period of 69 weeks (7 weeks plus 62 weeks) which equals 483 years.

- Verse 26 describes a period of time, or a gap, between the sixty-nine weeks and the seventieth week.
- Verse 27 then describes the fulfillment of the final week or period of seven years.

At some point in the future the final week (the final 7 years of the 490 year prophetic road map) will begin to unfold. Daniel's prophecy clearly inserts a gap between the sixty-ninth and seventieth weeks. During this time, Daniel tells us that the Messiah will be killed and Jerusalem will be destroyed. When we read the New Testament, we discover additional information about this gap of time.

The New Testament reveals that the Church Age fits within this gap of time between the sixty-ninth and seventieth weeks of Daniel. The Church was not directly predicted in the Old Testament. It is described as a *mystery*. The term *mystery* refers to previously unrevealed truth in God's plan. So although Daniel does not explicitly mention this new dispensation called *the Church*, the New Testament explains how and where the Church fits in God's timetable (Eph. 3:1-20). It is within this gap in Daniel's prophecy that we now live. God has suspended His 490 year plan for Israel for an unknown length of time as His attention shifts to the Church.

After the Church is removed at the Rapture, God's spotlight shifts once again to His chosen nation Israel.

After the Church is removed at the Rapture, God's spotlight shifts once again to His chosen nation Israel. The prophetic clock for Israel starts moving again. Daniel 9:27 reveals what will take place during this final seven years for Israel. It teaches, "Then he shall confirm a covenant with many for one week; but in the middle of the week he shall bring an end to sacrifice and offering. And on the wing of abominations shall be one who makes desolate, even until the consummation, which is determined, is poured out on the desolate" (Dan. 9:27).

The context of verse 26 dictates that the subject referred to in verse 27 is none other than the Antichrist. He will come to an agreement with the leaders of the world, but thankfully God will limit his rule to a period of seven years. At the midway point of this seven-year Tribulation the Antichrist will, "bring an end to sacrifice and offering" (Dan. 9:27). It will be at this time that he will break his peace treaty with Israel and end the worship of the Jews in the newly rebuilt Temple in Jerusalem. The end of verse 27 proclaims, "And on the wing of abominations shall be one who makes desolate, even until the consummation, which is determined, is poured out on the desolate." The Antichrist will declare his deity, set up his image in the Temple, and require the world to worship him. The New Testament confirms this incredible prophecy of the coming Tribulation (Matt. 25:15; 2 Thess. 2:3-4).

The Final Act

The Rapture is the next event on God's prophetic clock.

It is not for us to know when the final act in God's 490-year plan for Israel will begin. As time marches forward it is certain that every day brings us one more day closer to the Tribulation. The Rapture is the next event on God's prophetic clock. When the Lord Jesus returns for His Church, the events of Daniel 9:27, detailed in Revelation 4-19, will quickly begin to unfold. Even though periods of suffering will come, we recognize that God will use these terrible times as a part of His ultimate plan to bring Himself glory. This becomes our focus in chapter 5.

Discussion Questions – Chapter 4

1. Describe the significance of what happened to Jerusalem when Babylon besieged it.

2. What do we learn about Daniel, his character, and his faith from the Word of God?

3. What did Daniel learn while studying the words of Jeremiah? What was his reaction?

4. God revealed some important information to Daniel in the ninth chapter. What was it? Why is this revelation important?

5. How do we know there is a gap in time between the sixty-ninth and seventieth weeks? What occurs during this gap?

6. Describe the events that will occur during Daniel's Seventieth Week.

7. As time marches closer towards the Tribulation, what event can believers look forward to?

Endnotes - Chapter 4

1. Stephen R. Miller, vol. 18, *Daniel, The New American Commentary* (Nashville, TN: Broadman & Holman Publishers, 2001), 60.
2. Ibid., 240.

Chapter 5

A Glimpse of Glory

But he, being full of the Holy Spirit, gazed into heaven and saw the glory of God, and Jesus standing at the right hand of God, and said, "Look! I see the heavens opened and the Son of Man standing at the right hand of God!" - Acts 7:55-56

G reat strength is often demonstrated in ways we would not expect. It usually comes from the most unlikely people. Florence Chadwick was this type of person.

Growing up on the beaches of California had instilled within her a passion to swim. She started racing at the age of six, and by the time she was ten Chadwick had won her first competition. Her specialty was long distance swimming in rough water.

Swimming long distances in the ocean brings definite challenges. There is a constant conflict with the elements. Water temperatures, the burning sun, sharks, jellyfish, and the water currents are just a few of the battles that swimmers face, but Chadwick was well prepared. She took a job working for an oil company in Saudi Arabia and spent her free time training in the Persian Gulf. Then, after having successfully crossed the English Channel in 1950, her focus turned towards something else.

It was the fourth of July in 1952 and the target was the Catalina Channel. The distance for Chadwick to swim spanned twenty-one miles from Catalina Island to the California coast. This time, as she waded into the waters off of Catalina Island, she would not be breaking any records. The bitter cold water and the long distance to swim were only two of the obstacles she faced. Several times the sharks had to be fought off by men with rifles as they escorted her in boats, but the greatest enemy was one that was not seen as an immediate threat. The fog was so thick that she could hardly see the boats that guided her across the channel.

The repeated hours of swimming began to take their toll on her. The dense fog led to confusion and uncertainty. There was no way of knowing when they would reach land. Unable to see the coastline, she asked to be pulled out of the water after swimming for almost sixteen hours. Sitting in the boat, she discovered that she had stopped about a mile from shore. Being unable to see the coastline had led her to quit short of her goal. Neither the cold, exhaustion, or fear stopped her; it was the fog.

The Fog Has Rolled In

It is an unfortunate truth of living in a fallen world that men are often incapable of seeing the glory of God. The effects of sin have clouded our ability to recognize it. This fog has kept men from reaching the ultimate goal of living in fellowship with the Lord and understanding His plan for all of creation.

God alone is worthy of glory; this is an undisputed fact from Scripture. The record of creation found in Genesis reveals that God created mankind to live in fellowship with Him. Adam and Eve walked away from the glory of the Lord, ushering mankind into sin.

Even though the fog of sin rolled in, God did not abandon mankind.

The Apostle Paul teaches us, "Therefore, just as through one man sin entered the world, and death through sin, and thus death spread to all men, because all sinned" (Rom. 5:12).

Even though the fog of sin rolled in, God did not abandon mankind. His glory has been revealed to us in His creation, "The heavens declare the glory of God; and the firmament shows His handiwork" (Psa. 19:1). This is often referred to as the general revelation of God. God has declared His glory to all of mankind in

His creation. Paul referred to this in his letter to the church at Rome, "For since the creation of the world His invisible attributes are clearly seen, being understood by the things that are made, even His eternal power and Godhead, so that they are without excuse" (Rom. 1:20).

God has also declared His glory in the Scriptures. His written Word is referred to as the special revelation of God. To get a glimpse of the glory of God we turn our attention to Revelation 5, which is a description of a future scene in heaven when the newly glorified saints will join the angelic chorus praising Jesus Christ. What a celebration it will be! Notice the focus of the praise:

 And they sang a new song, saying: "You are worthy to take the scroll, and to open its seals; for You were slain, and have redeemed us to God by Your blood out of every tribe and tongue and people and nation, and have made us kings and priests to our God; and we shall reign on the earth." Then I looked, and I heard the voice of many angels around the throne, the living creatures, and the elders; and the number of them was ten thousand times ten thousand, and thousands of thousands, saying with a loud voice: "Worthy is the Lamb who was slain to receive power and riches and wisdom, and strength and honor and glory and blessing!" And every creature which is in heaven and on the earth and under the earth and such as are in the sea, and all that are in them, I heard saying: "Blessing and honor and glory and power be to Him who sits on the throne, and to the Lamb, forever and ever!" (Rev. 5:9-13).

Losing Sight of God's Glory and His Plan

The lies of Satan and the fall of mankind into sin have had a devastating effect on all of creation.

It is altogether easy in this present age to lose sight of God's glory and His plan for the ages. The lies of Satan and the fall of mankind into sin have had a devastating effect on all of creation. At present, Satan is the, "prince of the power of the air, the spirit who now works in the sons of disobedience" (Eph. 2:2). Yet, this does not mean that God has abdicated His sovereignty. He remains firmly in control.

As we look around us, it appears as though evil is proceeding unchecked. Injustice and heartache are everywhere. But we must never forget that God works out His plans in ways that are ultimately for our good and His glory (Rom. 8:28). At the same time, however, we must keep our eyes wide open to what Satan is trying to do in this age.

Imagine a missionary in a foreign land returning from several days of ministry in the jungle only to discover a twenty-foot python in his hut. Immediately, he pulls out his pistol and shoots the python through the head. It is a fatal wound, but the huge snake continues to thrash around for several minutes. For his own safety, the missionary chooses to wait outside. When all sounds quiet, he steps back into his hut. Tables are overturned, lamps and dishes are broken, and his cooking pots are scattered. The python is dead, but the hut is in shambles.

We dare not overlook the deception of Satan in this present evil age. Still, the worst is yet to come.

In the same manner, Satan received his fatal blow at Calvary. He is defeated, but he still thrashes around from his mortal wound. It is his plan to drag as many people as possible into judgment with him. Satan destroys homes and ruins lives. He will wreck a church from the inside out if given the chance. It is for this reason that Peter warned, "Be sober, be vigilant; because your adversary the devil walks about like a roaring lion, seeking whom he may devour" (1 Pet. 5:8). We dare not overlook the deception of Satan in this present evil age. Still, the worst is yet to come.

Thickening Fog

The deception and work of Satan will greatly intensify during the future seven-year Tribulation period. Jesus warned that during this time, "false christs and false prophets will rise and show great signs and wonders to deceive, if possible, even the elect" (Matt. 24:24). These unrelenting forces will operate under the power of Satan. All of their words and actions will be calculated to deceive every person possible.

Paul addressed the devastating time to come in his second letter to the Thessalonians. Notice how Paul began to address this topic, "Now, brethren, concerning the coming of our Lord Jesus Christ and our gathering together to Him, we ask you, not to be soon shaken in mind or troubled, either by spirit or by word or by letter, as if from us, as though the day of Christ had come" (2 Thess. 2:1-2). The gathering together that Paul mentioned was a reference to the Rapture of the Church. The situation they faced may be hard for us to imagine. The persecution that the first century Christians at Thessalonica endured was so intense it left them with the questions, "Has the day of the Lord arrived? Are we already in the Tribulation?" To make matters worse, apparently someone had forged a letter and signed Paul's name. This letter had incorrectly announced that the Tribulation had begun.

There was no need to panic. Paul proclaimed, "Let no one deceive you by any means; for that Day will not come unless the falling away comes first, and the man of sin is revealed, the son of perdition, who opposes and exalts himself above all that is called God or that is worshiped, so that he sits as God in the temple of God, showing himself that he is God" (2 Thess. 2:3-4). Paul listed two things that must happen before the day of Christ. Paul mentioned, "the falling away comes first" (2 Thess. 2:3).

The expression *falling away* is the Greek word *apostasia*. It carries the literal meaning of *departure*. As with all words, context governs meaning. In the English language, apostasy has become synonymous with spiritual departure from the faith by the acceptance of false doctrine. Yet, the context in this case suggests that Paul used the word to refer to a physical departure. In fact, verse 1 speaks of the physical departure of the Church to meet the Lord at Christ's return. Paul had previously instructed the Thessalonians about this movement of Christians from the earth to the sky where they will meet the Lord in the air (1 Thess. 4:13-18). Thus, when a departure is mentioned again in verse 3, it is most natural to see this as a physical departure not a spiritual falling away. The departure mentioned in verse 3 is a reference to the gathering of believers to Christ, the Rapture of the Church.

The second reason Paul had stated that the Thessalonians could be certain they were not in the Tribulation was because the man of sin had not yet been revealed. Paul also referred to this man as, "the son of perdition" (2 Thess. 2:3). This is the Antichrist, who will demand to be worshipped. The newly rebuilt Temple in Jerusalem will be transformed into a place where the world will be required to worship the Antichrist.

Like the Thessalonians, we too can conclude that we are not in the Tribulation because neither of these two events has occurred. The Rapture has not taken place and the Antichrist has not been unveiled. This passage is one of the strongest texts in the New Testament declaring the pre-tribulation Rapture of the Church.

This was not new information for the Christians at Thessalonica. Paul instructed, "Do you not remember that when I was still with you I told you these things? And now you know what is restraining, that he may be revealed in his own time. For the mystery of lawlessness is already at work; only He who now restrains will do so until He is taken out of the way" (2 Thess. 2:5-7).

In verse 7 we again witness the consistency of Scripture. Paul directly stated that, "the mystery of lawlessness is already at work" (2 Thess. 2:7). Once more, this takes us to the teaching of 1 John 2:18 where we have witnessed that many agents of deception are already present in this world.

At the point of verse 6, we are told that someone or something is restraining or holding back the appearance of the Antichrist. Verse 7 identifies the restrainer as a person, "only He who now restrains will do so until He is taken out of the way" (2 Thess. 2:7). The right question to ask is, "What person all by himself is capable of restraining or holding back the appearing of the Antichrist?" There is only one answer, God. Specifically, the reference is to the restraining power of the Holy Spirit within the Body of Christ.

Let us be clear about the teaching of this text. This is not referring to the complete removal of the presence of the Holy Spirit from this

Right now every believer in Christ is permanently indwelt by the Spirit of God—one of the unique blessings of the present Church Age.

world at the Rapture. The Holy Spirit is God and God is omnipresent, which simply means that He is present everywhere at all times. To say that God will not be present on earth during the Tribulation would be to deny the very truth of who God is.

Right now every believer in Christ is permanently indwelt by the Spirit of God—one of the unique blessings of the present Church Age. When the Church is raptured, the instant removal of every Christian on the face of the earth will take away the restraining influence of God's people who are operating under the power of the Holy Spirit. Notice again, that another physical departure is emphasized. This theme of departure runs throughout the passage.

After the Church is taken out of the way we are told:

> And then the lawless one will be revealed, whom the Lord will consume with the breath of His mouth and destroy with the brightness of His coming. The coming of the lawless one is according to the working of Satan, with all power, signs, and lying wonders, and with all unrighteous deception among those who perish, because they did not receive the love of the truth, that they might be saved (2 Thess. 2:8-10).

This will be when the Antichrist steps into the public arena. Take note that Paul skips ahead to Christ's Second Coming to the earth at the end of the Tribulation when he proclaims, "whom the Lord will consume with the breath of His mouth and destroy with the brightness of His coming" (2 Thess. 2:8). Paul juxtaposes the coming of the Antichrist with the coming of the Lord to restore order and justice and peace to the world. Jesus Christ will completely overwhelm Satan and his followers. Satan has no chance of winning in the end.

Verse 9 seems to suggest that the Antichrist will be indwelt by Satan. At the very least, he will be empowered by Satan (Rev. 13:2). This satanic power will give him the ability to perform miracles, which will sway the masses of humanity to worship and follow him. If these people would respond with faith to the Gospel of Christ they would not have to fall into this coming deception (2 Thess. 2:10).

Pay careful attention to the teaching that follows, "And for this reason God will send them strong delusion, that they should believe the lie" (2 Thess. 2:11). The opening words of this verse tie directly back to verse 10. The reason God will send them a strong delusion is because of their rejection of Jesus Christ and His redemptive sacrifice. Jesus Himself testified, "I am the way, the truth, and the life. No one comes to the Father except through Me" (John 14:6). Only those who receive this truth will be saved (2 Thess. 2:10).

It would be easy to overlook another aspect of verse 11. A strong delusion will lead those who rejected Christ to "believe the lie" of the Antichrist (2 Thess. 2:11). Some understand this to be teaching that every person who rejects Jesus Christ before the Rapture will be unable to believe in Christ afterwards. According to this view, the great multitudes of people from every nation, tribe, tongue, and language who trust Christ and are saved during the Tribulation are those who never heard the gospel prior to the Rapture. Others understand verse 11 to refer to those who reject Christ during the Tribulation and seal their doom by taking the mark of the beast. Either way, Satan's deception will be even more pervasive than it is today. Remember, Satan's deception has been growing worse and worse for the last 2,000 years (2 Tim. 3:13).

At its core, verse 11 reminds us of a significant truth. Great numbers of people will continue to be blinded to the schemes of Satan, but this is all part of God's plan. Most certainly God did not cause Satan to rebel, but He did allow it for His greater purpose. In the same manner, God did not cause Adam and Eve to fall into sin in Genesis 3, but once again He allowed it to happen. God has given free

68

will to mankind and to the angels. He knew what Satan and Adam would do before they did! None of it caught God off guard because He has always known these things.

Rejecting the truth of Jesus Christ has eternal consequences.

Speaking of those who will believe the lie Paul testifies, "that they all may be condemned who did not believe the truth but had pleasure in unrighteousness" (2 Thess. 2:12). Rejecting the truth of Jesus Christ has eternal consequences. Those who buy Satan's temporary substitute (the pleasures of sin) will regret their purchase for all of eternity. The writer of Hebrews refers to Satan's counterfeit as, "the passing pleasures of sin" (Heb. 11:25). For those who live with little regard for eternal truth, Satan's lies can be seductive and powerful. This is why he is able to deceive, "the whole world" (Rev. 12:9).

The time is coming when the satanic deception will lead to the worship of the Antichrist by, "those who dwell on the earth" (Rev. 13:14). However, we must never forget that Satan will not win in the end. His days are numbered and his future is determined. We can look forward to the day when, "The devil, who deceived them, was cast into the lake of fire and brimstone where the beast and the false prophet are. And they will be tormented day and night forever and ever" (Rev. 20:10).

The Fog Will Lift

God's end times plan will ultimately give Him eternal glory. Our Creator and Sustainer is worthy of this glory. Despite the efforts of Satan to corrupt everything he can in this fallen world, God will ultimately conquer Satan by His sovereign power and redemptive grace.

Take a look at figure 5.1. Both God's creative and redemptive work fulfills His plans. Starting at the bottom left we see that God created the universe, the nations, Israel, and His Church.

Figure 5.1[1]

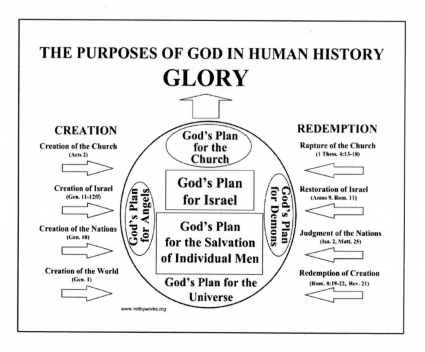

THE PURPOSES OF GOD IN HUMAN HISTORY

GLORY

CREATION

Creation of the Church
(Acts 2)

Creation of Israel
(Gen. 11-12ff)

Creation of the Nations
(Gen. 10)

Creation of the World
(Gen. 1)

God's Plan for Angels

God's Plan
for the
Church

God's Plan
for Israel

God's Plan
for the Salvation
of Individual Men

God's Plan for the
Universe

God's Plan for Demons

REDEMPTION

Rapture of the Church
(1 Thess. 4:13-18)

Restoration of Israel
(Amos 9, Rom. 11)

Judgment of the Nations
(Isa. 2, Matt. 25)

Redemption of Creation
(Rom. 8:19-22, Rev. 21)

www.notbyworks.org

Satan's rebellion and the fall of man have had a devastating effect on creation. God is at work carrying out His plans, which includes so much more than just the redemption of men. Working our way down the column on the right we see that God has a plan for His Church, Israel, the nations, and the redemption of all of creation. God even has a plan for the angels and the demons. His redemptive plan is working out all these things for His glory.

God is busy working to redeem and restore His creation. His plan for the universe is right on schedule.

We can take confidence from knowing that while we are immersed in the fog of this world God is busy working to redeem and restore His creation. His plan for the universe is right on schedule. The psalmist tells us, "Let them praise the name of the LORD, for His name alone is exalted; His glory is above the earth and heaven" (Psa. 148:13). Instead of embracing despair over the rebellion of men we can rejoice with the Apostle Paul in proclaiming, "Oh, the depth of the riches both of the wisdom and knowledge of God! How unsearchable are His judgments and His ways past finding out!" (Rom. 11:33). Right now we can only see a shadow of what lies ahead in the future, but nevertheless our confidence remains steadfast with the Lord. Next, we take a look at why all of this matters.

Discussion Questions – Chapter 5

1. Why are men often incapable of seeing the glory of God?

2. How does God proclaim His glory?

3. What is Satan's goal in the world today?

4. What will happen with the deception of Satan over time?

5. List some of the purposes of God that He is working to accomplish in His plan for the end times.

6. Why should we have confidence even though we are living within the fog of deception?

Endnotes - Chapter 5

1. This chart has been adapted from Mike Stallard at Baptist Bible Seminary, Clarks Summit, PA.

Chapter 6

Deception Among Us

For I know this, that after my departure savage wolves will come in among you, not sparing the flock. Also from among yourselves men will rise up, speaking perverse things, to draw away the disciples after themselves. - Acts 20:29-30

Nobody wants to go to a dying church, but sometimes this can take on a whole new meaning. For a large church in California, this is the road they found themselves on.

It was hard to dispute their record because their accomplishments were many. A heated swimming pool and riding horses were provided for underprivileged kids. Scholarships were given to students, and housing was arranged for senior citizens. The list of achievements included an animal shelter, a medical facility, and a drug rehabilitation program. Counseling was offered to prisoners. A job placement center was opened and free legal aid was given. National figures and leading politicians heaped up public words of praise for the pastor of this church. This was a place that offered people the hope they were looking for. It stunned the world when the congregation died all at once.

In 1977 Jim Jones moved his congregation to the jungles of Guyana to a home that became known to the world as Jonestown. This agricultural commune was promised to be a utopia nestled into the wilderness of South America. Instead, it became a death camp.

Jones publically stated that he was the reincarnation of Jesus. Behind closed doors he was a committed communist who used religion as a method for social change. His thirst for power led to a brutal clampdown on the people of Jonestown. Passports and money were removed from them, leaving little opportunity to escape. His followers were forced to stage rehearsals for a mass suicide.

Rumors of the cult had spread to the United States, which led U.S. Representative Leo Ryan to investigate the compound. He arrived with reporters, and concerned family members of the Jonestown people, on November 14, 1978. Fourteen members of the cult decided to defect. Four days later, as the group decided to leave, Jones ordered for them all to be assassinated. Since most of the delegation escaped the assassination attempt, Jones activated his suicide plan.

The people of Jonestown were called to assemble at the pavilion. The voice of their pastor spoke to them over the speaker system. From all four corners of the compound the people came. Jones sat in his large chair speaking into a microphone about the beauty of death. Containers of punch laced with cyanide were brought out, and the people were commanded to drink. The few that tried to resist were forced to obey. The poison was handed out in order; babies first, children next, followed by the women, and then finally the men.

There were a few minutes of calm, but then the seizures began. Horrible screams of desperation filled the air as chaos broke out. Within a few short minutes it was over. The members of the Peoples Temple Christian Church were dead. The final death toll was placed at 918 souls that lost their lives on that day, including hundreds of children. Jim Jones died of a gunshot wound to the head.[1]

This type of disturbing event is not an isolated case. David Koresh of the Branch Davidians also claimed to be the Messiah, and deceived a number of followers. The FBI's ill-fated and unprovoked raid on the Branch Davidian compound in Waco, Texas in 1993 led to the deaths of seventy-six people.

In more recent headlines we read of Warren Jeffs of the Fundamentalist Church of Jesus Christ of Latter-Day Saints. This particular group holds to the original teaching of Latter-Day Saints (Mormons) regarding polygamy. Jeffs took leadership of the group in 2002 when his father died, taking his father's wives as his own. This cult leader took control over a number of women and young girls. His revolting crimes against them led to his arrest and incarceration.

The lessons that come from these examples are substantial. They illustrate that you can claim to be a fundamentalist, but lack the doctrines of Christ. Together they stand as a warning that there are great dangers in following a man in place of the Lord Jesus Christ. The doctrines of demons usually espouse the belief in the return of a messiah, but it is a false messiah. This type of theology comes straight from the pits of hell.

False teachers normally have a pattern. They are greedy, man-centered, and will feed you promises and a lifestyle that is completely opposed to Jesus Christ. These type of men never seem to have a problem gaining an audience because there will always be plenty of people that are desperate enough to believe their lies. These smooth talkers promise freedom, but deliver slavery. They speak with familiar words to entrap people with their lies of destruction.

Even more concerning than the cults, are the false teachers that have infiltrated the Church of Jesus Christ, proclaiming man-centered theology in order to gain a crowd.

Even more concerning than the cults, are the false teachers that have infiltrated the Church of Jesus Christ, proclaiming man-centered theology in order to gain a crowd. They tickle the ears of Christians instead of exhorting men and women to follow Jesus Christ.

The point is to recognize that deception is already ever-present in this fallen world. Understanding the sequential order of the events of the end times can lead to the incorrect assumption that the Church is immune to Satan's deception. It is sometimes suggested that if the pre-tribulation Rapture of the Church is correct then, "Why is Satan's plan for global deception relevant to us? Church Age believers in Christ will not be here when the Tribulation happens, so why should we care what the Antichrist is going to do? How does this affect us?"

The Great Deceiver

Looking ahead at the deception that will come helps us to recognize the deception that is already taking place right now. Satan's larger scheme alerts us to the dangers of his ongoing plans in this world. His overall method has not changed; he continues to do what he has done in the past. Satan tempts us with the same temptations he used on Eve (cf., Gen. 3:6 and 1 John 2:16). We can know from the Word of God that the type of deception he plans to carry out during the end times is also a part of his plot for these last days. We must not be ignorant of his devices (2 Cor. 2:11).

Satan is not going to deceive the world one day; he is deceiving the world today.

We have already witnessed that throughout the Church Age, "evil men and impostors will grow worse and worse, deceiving and being deceived" (2 Tim. 3:13). This incremental increase means that deception is more prevalent today than at any other time in history. Satan is not going to deceive the world *one day*; he is deceiving the world *today*. This is his normal mode of operation.

There can be no question that Satan's deception is a theme that runs from Genesis to Revelation. For mankind, it began in the garden when Satan deceived Eve. She had correctly stated that they were not to eat of the tree of the knowledge of good and evil (Gen. 2:17; 3:3). The serpent contradicted the Creator when he said, "You will not surely die. For God knows that in the day you eat of it your eyes will be opened, and you will be like God, knowing good and evil" (Gen. 3:4-5).

The seed of temptation had been planted. The tree and its fruit were now desirable to Eve. She ate the fruit and gave some to Adam (Gen. 3:6). Their innocence was gone; sin had now entered the world (Rom. 5:12).

Adam and Eve still had to face their Creator. When Eve's turn came to face God, He said to her, "What is this you have done?" (Gen. 3:13). Eve attempted to deflect personal responsibility. She said, "The serpent deceived me, and I ate" (Gen. 3:13). She stated the truth, but it did not excuse her sin. Adam, Eve, and the serpent were judged (Gen. 3:14-19). Before a holy God, they stood guilty.

Thousands of years later the problem persists. In the Church Age we have the benefit of being indwelt by the Holy Spirit. Still, Paul found it necessary to warn, "I fear, lest somehow, as the serpent deceived Eve by his craftiness, so your minds may be corrupted from the simplicity that is in Christ" (2 Cor. 11:3). The Apostle Paul recognized the need to be alert to Satan's deception.

Satan has been at it a long time. He is, "that serpent of old, called the Devil and Satan, who deceives the whole world" (Rev. 12:9). He works actively to, "deceive the nations" (Rev. 20:3).

It is a glorious truth of Scripture that during the Millennium Satan will be bound. The Millennium refers to that future one thousand year period following the Second Coming when Christ will unseat the Antichrist and rule and reign in perfect peace, justice, and righteousness. Christ will not allow Satan's deception to continue. He will no longer be the god of this world or the prince of the power of the air. Instead, he will be restrained. In Revelation, John described what he saw:

> Then I saw an angel coming down from heaven, having the key to the bottomless pit and a great chain in his hand. He laid hold of the dragon, that serpent of old, who is the Devil and Satan, and bound him for a thousand years; and he cast him into the bottomless pit, and shut him up, and set a seal on him, so that he should deceive the nations no more till the thousand years were finished. But after these things he must be released for a little while (Rev. 20:1-3).

Being bound for one thousand years will not rehabilitate Satan. Upon his release he, "will go out to deceive the nations which are in the four corners of the earth" (Rev. 20:8). It is hard to fathom, but once again Satan will win a crowd, "whose number is as the sand of the sea" (Rev. 20:8). The deception will be short lived because God will crush the rebellion (Rev. 20:9). The final judgment will be executed upon the great deceiver, "The devil, who deceived them, was cast into the lake of fire and brimstone where the beast and the false prophet are. And they will be tormented day and night forever and ever" (Rev. 20:10). Until then, deception will continue.

The Deceived: Outside the Church

It should not be a great surprise to many Christians that there is widespread deception taking place outside the Church of Jesus Christ. We remember that the Apostle Paul taught, "If our gospel is veiled, it is veiled to those who are perishing, whose minds the god of this age has blinded, who do not believe, lest the light of the gospel of the glory of Christ, who is the image of God, should shine on them" (2 Cor. 4:3-4). Satan seeks to drag as many people as possible into eternal condemnation.

There is a method to the Devil's madness. It is instructive to read, "For all that is in the world—the lust of the flesh, the lust of the eyes, and the pride of life—is not of the Father but is of the world" (1 John 2:16). Satan appeals to these appetites to lead people into deception.

The pride of life is both dangerous and destructive. Satan is no fool; his method is to use people by appealing to their own pride. Such a man is, "vainly puffed up by his fleshly mind" (Col. 2:18). It is this type of imprudence that leads men to believe that they are capable of leading others astray without falling into the same traps of deception themselves. Yet, as we have witnessed, God's Word teaches otherwise. They are, "deceiving and being deceived" (2 Tim. 3:13). This is all a part of Satan's strategy.

The lust of the flesh is another powerful weakness that he can exploit. Satan uses this to appeal to an individual's passions. The Apostle Paul described unbelievers when he warned, "Do not be deceived. Neither fornicators, nor idolaters, nor adulterers, nor homosexuals, nor sodomites ... will inherit the kingdom of God" (1 Cor. 6:9-10). These people celebrate their freedom while going deeper into bondage (Rom. 1:22-32). The widespread perversion in our culture confirms the predicted deception of our time.

The Deceived: Inside the Church

Of greater concern is the deception that runs rampant within the Church of Jesus Christ. There is a reason Christians are all too familiar with the lies of Satan. Consider the words from the Apostle Paul on this matter, "For we ourselves were also once foolish, disobedient, deceived, serving various lusts and pleasures, living in malice and envy, hateful and hating one another" (Titus 3:3). After salvation in Christ, our fallen natures remain alive and well. False doctrine appeals to our old nature.

After salvation in Christ, our fallen natures remain alive and well. False doctrine appeals to our old nature.

False doctrine can certainly confuse believers. Paul instructed the church at Colossae to be vigilant, "lest anyone should deceive you with persuasive words" (Col. 2:4). Regarding the doctrines of the end times, this was the same concern that the Apostle had for the church at Thessalonica. Paul wrote, "Let no one deceive you by any means..." (2 Thess. 2:3).

Battling deception has been a continual struggle for the Church of Jesus Christ. Reading the epistles of Paul in the New Testament reveals that he saw this as a great problem. He warned Timothy, "Now the Spirit expressly says that in latter times some will depart from the faith, giving heed to deceiving spirits and doctrines of demons, speaking lies in hypocrisy, having their own conscience seared with a hot iron" (1 Tim. 4:1-2).

The dangerous lies propagated by false teachers encourage believers to sin. The Apostle John recognized this when he stated, "Little children, let no one deceive you. He who practices righteousness is righteous, just as He is righteous" (1 John 3:7). It is inconsistent with our relationship with Christ to live in unrighteousness. Paul had even stronger words concerning this when he proclaimed, "Let no one deceive you with empty words, for because of these things the wrath of God comes upon the sons of disobedience. Therefore do not be partakers with them" (Eph. 5:6-7).

Deception is not limited to the satanic forces of this world. Christians tend to be unaware of the possibility of deceiving themselves. Perhaps this is where the greatest danger is.

We can deceive ourselves about our own sin. John warned, "If we say that we have no sin, we deceive ourselves, and the truth is not in us" (1 John 1:8). James actually warned several times about the danger of self-deception. Regarding the dangers of sin we are told, "Then, when desire has conceived, it gives birth to sin; and sin, when it is full-grown, brings forth death. Do not be deceived, my beloved brethren" (James 1:15-16). James also cautioned about the pitfall of failing to live out the Word of God when he stated, "But be doers of the word, and not hearers only, deceiving yourselves" (James 1:22).

It is also possible to deceive ourselves regarding our own walk with Christ. This is what James was getting at when he said, "If anyone among you thinks he is religious, and does not bridle his tongue but deceives his own heart, this one's religion is useless" (James 1:26).

Pride is a deceptive enemy for believers. Arrogance leads us to the belief that we are better than our brothers and sisters in Christ. In turn, this leads Christians to judge one another. Paul correctly taught, "For if anyone thinks himself to be something, when he is nothing, he deceives himself" (Gal. 6:3).

Just a few verses later Paul continued his warnings about self-deception. This time he said, "Do not be deceived, God is not mocked; for whatever a man sows, that he will also reap. For he who sows to his flesh will of the flesh reap corruption, but he who sows to the Spirit will of the Spirit reap everlasting life" (Gal. 6:7-8). Paul was once again sounding the alarm over the dangers of sin.

Christians have a tendency to excuse away our own behavior.

Christians have a tendency to excuse away our own behavior. Consider the church at Corinth; they faced a number of problems. Among them, the Christians remained in continued fellowship with men and women living immoral lives. Furthermore, they seemed to have no trouble listening to men who proclaimed doctrines contrary to Christ. Paul taught them, "Do not be deceived: 'Evil company corrupts good habits'" (1 Cor. 15:33).

The Tactics of Satan

Satan's goal is to turn as many people as he can away from God.

Satan's goal is to turn as many people as he can away from God. How does he accomplish this? Some of his schemes, like the occult, should be obvious to believers in Christ. Other tactics used by Satan are much more subtle. Therefore, it is critical that as believers we understand what the schemes of Satan are so that we can, "resist the devil" (James 4:7) throughout our Christian walk. In the next chapter we will highlight some of the prominent tactics Satan uses today to accomplish his goal of deceiving the world.

Discussion Questions – Chapter 6

1. Why should Church Age believers be concerned about the deception of Satan?

2. Name one example of how Satan deceived people in the Bible.

3. What are some examples of what Satan uses to entice people?

4. Are Christians immune to the deception of Satan? Explain.

5. Can we deceive ourselves? If so, how do we do this?

Endnotes - Chapter 6

1. The story of the Jonestown massacre is a fascinating study for those with the time and inclination to look beyond the accepted version. As with most historical events, there are many details and aspects of this horrific event that are not widely known.

Chapter 7

Anatomy of Deception

The simple believes every word, but the prudent considers well his steps. - Proverbs 14:15

The loss of a great leader breaks the heart of a nation. The tragic death of President Abraham Lincoln on April 15, 1865 was a profound blow to citizens of the northern United States. A funeral train proceeded through the northern cities of the nation carrying his body, and hundreds of thousands of people came out to mourn the loss of their president.

What happened next could not have been predicted. No one would have guessed after the funeral that his coffin would be moved a total of seventeen times throughout the years. It would have been inconceivable to think that the coffin itself would be opened at least five times.[1] On a few occasions, his body was actually transferred to a different coffin. Even though he was dead, President Lincoln was on the move.

The last two times his coffin was opened the caretakers of his grave checked to make sure that it was actually his body inside. Rumors of Lincoln's body not being in his coffin had made their way throughout the land. To many people it was an accepted truth that Lincoln's body was not where it was supposed to be.

Therefore, in 1887 the coffin was opened, and eighteen people filed past to witness the corpse. This was twenty-two years after his assassination. Every witness testified that it was in fact the body of the former President of the United States. Lincoln was once again laid to rest.

By 1901, the rumors were again sweeping throughout the land. Even though the coffin had been opened only fourteen years before, it was considered common knowledge that Abraham Lincoln was not really in his coffin. People kept accepting it as truth. The more the lie was repeated, the more it was believed by the citizens of the United States.

The decision was made to open the casket one final time. Lincoln was now in a lead-lined coffin. Two plumbers chiseled out a section just over Lincoln's head and shoulders. As soon as the hole was opened a harsh choking smell poured out of the coffin. Twenty-three people took turns looking into the opening, just to make sure it was him.

According to their testimony, even though it had been thirty-six years since he was killed, his facial features had not changed much at all. His hair, beard, and mole on his face were all still there. Lincoln still had the same suit on, but it was now covered with yellow mold. His eyebrows had fallen off and his gloves had rotted onto his hands, but it most certainly was the body of President Abraham Lincoln. It has been speculated that the frequent embalming while his body was on the funeral train led to a corpse that is practically mummified.

To make sure none of this would ever happen again, the casket was soldered back together and placed into a steel cage. Then, 4,000 pounds of concrete were poured to encase both the cage and the casket. The body of President Abraham Lincoln has not been moved since.

Each time a lie is repeated it is given new life. Deception does not have to be forceful; it can be subtle. Quite often the accepted truth of humanity differs greatly from the reality on the ground. It becomes difficult to know the truth in a culture operating on lies.

As we witnessed in chapter 6, deception can be traced all the way back to the Garden of Eden. It is instructive to look more in depth at Satan's deceptive approach to God's Word because it demonstrates to us his pattern of twisting the truth. He continues to use the same method because it still works. Notice five core essentials of deception in the original story in Genesis 3.

Question Truth

The very first thing that Satan did was question God's truth, "Now the serpent was more cunning than any beast of the field which the LORD God had made. And he said to the woman, 'Has God indeed said, "You shall not eat of every tree of the garden"?'" (Gen. 3:1).

Certain things are true for all people, in all places, at all times. Truth is absolute, not relative.

There is a great need for clarity on this point. Almost everyone has times of questioning and searching for truth. We should ask the tough questions, but we must approach our quest with the understanding that absolute truth exists. Certain things are true for all people, in all places, at all times. Truth is absolute, not relative. We can know God's truth by looking to His Word. As the Proverb states, "I may make you know the certainty of the words of truth, that you may answer words of truth to those who send to you" (Prov. 22:21).

When we look to the Psalms we find David asking some deep, dark, troubling questions because he was seeking answers from God.

A faith that will not stand the test of time, or scrutiny from a troubled heart and a doubting mind, is not worth having.

A mere seven verses into the book of Psalms David asked, "Why do the nations rage, and the people plot a vain thing?" (Psa. 2:1). This is the type of question that any one of us could ask after reading the morning news.

Every Christian has the right to pray and search God's Word for answers to life's troubling issues. A faith that will not stand the test of time, or scrutiny from a troubled heart and a doubting mind, is not worth having. God welcomes the questions of His people. He cares about the things that trouble you. Nothing that we might ask could ever stump God.

But Satan's question was different because it was not an honest search for truth. It was a question designed to deceive. It was a question with a nefarious motive. This was an attack on truth because Satan questioned God's Word.

Misrepresent Truth

The second tactic Satan employed was to misrepresent God's truth. Notice again the words spoken to Eve, "Has God indeed said, 'You shall not eat of every tree of the garden'?" (Gen. 3:1). Satan was not seeking information. Instead, he misrepresented the truth he already knew.

The instruction from God to Adam was clear, "Of every tree of the garden you may freely eat; but of the tree of the knowledge of good and evil you shall not eat, for in the day that you eat of it you shall surely die" (Gen. 2:16-17). There was no ambiguity about God's directions. There was an abundance of food for Adam and Eve to enjoy. Only the fruit of one tree was off the menu. Disobedience would bring disastrous consequences.

To hear Satan tell it, God had severely limited what Adam and Eve could eat. This subtle twist of the truth is one of the weapons in Satan's arsenal. The most effective lies are always laced with traces of truth.

Contradict Truth

Satan is not content merely to distort the truth. There are times when Satan directly contradicts the truth. God had specifically said, "In the day that you eat of it you shall surely die" (Gen. 2:17). With profound arrogance Satan asserted, "You will not surely die" (Gen. 3:4). The Lord Jesus indicated that Satan, "does not stand in the truth, because there is no truth in him. When he speaks a lie, he speaks from his own resources, for he is a liar and the father of it" (John 8:44).

Focus on Motives

Satan had launched an assault on the truth in the Garden of Eden, but he was not done yet. His next trick was to focus on motives rather than substance. Satan stated, "For God knows that in the day you eat of it your eyes will be opened, and you will be like God, knowing good and evil" (Gen. 3:5).

Deception always has an agenda.

He directly questioned God's motives and intentions. The Devil made himself the arbiter of the thoughts of God. Satan presumed to tell Eve what God really meant when He said not to eat from the tree of the knowledge of good and evil. Deception always has an agenda. In this case, one of Satan's objectives was to undermine confidence in God.

This approach is the essence of our postmodern culture. People no longer concern themselves with the substance of what someone says or writes. The focus is on the perceived motive of the speaker or writer. Perception has become more important than reality, and speculation trumps empirical evidence. The makeup artist is valued more highly in our culture than the speechwriter. The stage manager outranks the copyeditor. This leads to the biggest lie in Satan's bag of deceptions.

Deconstruct Language

The fifth tactic used by Satan in the Garden of Eden was to deconstruct language. He redefined what God had plainly said to suit his own needs. We have already witnessed that God had stated, "In the day that you eat of it you shall surely die" (Gen. 2:17). In contrast, "The serpent said to the woman, 'You will not surely die.' For God knows that in the day you eat of it your eyes will be opened, and you will be like God, knowing good and evil" (Gen. 3:4-5). Satan contradicted God's warning, besmirched God's motives, and assigned new meaning to God's words. Satan's message to Eve was that when God said you will die, He really meant that He does not want you to be like Him and know what He knows. What a lie!

Satan is a classic deconstructionist. One expert defines deconstructionism as follows:

 Deconstructionism strips reality and written texts of inherent meaning. It reduces language to but a social construct mirroring the interpreter's personal perspective. Consequently, every interpreter is free to handle the text selectively, that is, to deconstruct it, and to refashion favored segments into fresh readings that reflect one's own preferences without evident anchorage in the text.[2]

In other words, meaning now resides with the listener or reader. Each person determines what the words mean based on feelings and impressions. A deconstructionist does not seek meaning in the original intent of the words used by the author or speaker. This is precisely what Satan did; he deconstructed God's language. Satan told Eve what God *really* meant.

Friedrich Nietzsche, a famous atheistic philosopher, said, "I fear we are not getting rid of God because we still believe in grammar."[3] When words lose their inherent meaning we have no way to discover truth.

Plainly, Satan has deceived our culture into embracing this lie. Students are given credit for answering 2 + 2 = 5 because:

- the student thought the teacher meant 2 + 3
- the student tried hard and we must not hurt his or her feelings
- the student feels that 5 is the correct answer for him-or herself as an individual

Deconstructionism was on full display when a recent President of the United States claimed that his false testimony to a Grand Jury was actually true, depending on one's definition of *is*. Yet another President stated after ten days of bombing sorties and missile attacks on Libya, by U.S. aircraft carriers and warships, that we were not participating in a war, but a *kinetic military action*. In so doing, he was able to circumvent the constitutional requirement for Congressional approval prior to launching war.

Deconstructionism is present in the modern day attacks against the U.S. Constitution, as well as in feminist and liberation theologies. We have ceased to communicate and have now embraced chaos. Ambiguity wins out over certainty every time because it leaves wiggle room to advance one's personal, self-serving agenda. Nietzsche was on to something: when words no longer have meaning, the end of life as we know it cannot be far behind.

> *We have ceased to communicate and have now embraced chaos.*

Time to Wake Up

Having examined the anatomy of deception, we turn next to some of the manifestations of his agenda in contemporary society. Knowing his methods, we should be better equipped to identify his lies when we see them. Still, this is where the principle of 2 Timothy 3:13 really begins to play out. The world has experienced 2,000 years of intensification in deception. The result is that, for many people, the common view of reality may not be accurate at all. The next chapter is sure to be the most controversial in this book. But if you read it with an open mind, and do your own research, you will awaken to a reality you never knew existed, and thus be better equipped to navigate the deceptive days ahead.

Discussion Questions – Chapter 7

1. What is the first thing Satan did when he sought to deceive Eve?

2. What makes a lie most effective?

3. How did Satan directly contradict God's Word in the Garden?

4. How does Satan try to undermine God?

5. What is the biggest lie in Satan's bag of deceptions today?

6. Define deconstructionism.

7. As Christians awaken to the truth, what will happen?

Endnotes - Chapter 7

1. Reports differ between Lincoln's coffins being opened a total of five or six times.
2. Carl F. H. Henry, "Postmodernism: The New Spectre?" in *The Challenge of Postmodernism: An Evangelical Engagement*, ed. David S. Dockery (Wheaton, IL: Victor Books, 1995), 39.
3. This quote is widely attributed to Nietzsche in various writings.

Chapter 8

Top Ten Lies Impacting the World Today

The coming of the lawless one is according to the working of Satan, with all power, signs, and lying wonders.

- 2 Thessalonians 2:9

A good rule of thumb in this age of deception is this: question everything. Almost nothing is really as it seems.

The lies of Satan are not limited to mere theological or philosophical discussions. They have very real implications. His fabrications have swept the globe and continue to dominate the headlines of our time. These lies serve to advance his agenda in very direct ways. Even many Christians have become unwitting and unknowing captives of Satan's global deceptive scheme. A good rule of thumb in this age of deception is this: question everything. Almost nothing is really as it seems.

The onset of postmodernity brought with it the death of *truth* and replaced it with the governing principle of *perception*. You can be sure that if you read it in a mainstream publication, or watch it on a mainstream news program, or listen to it on a mainstream radio program, it is certain to contain agenda-driven propaganda. If information comes to you, rather than you seeking it out yourself, it came to you for a reason. Consider ten of Satan's more recent lies that have become accepted as true by our mainstream culture.

Lie #1: Darwinism is a legitimate science.

Contrary to the popular understanding, Charles Darwin was not a scientist. He was a eugenicist. Eugenics is a core principle in Satan's agenda to take over the world. Eugenics refers to the study of hereditary improvement of the human race by controlled selective breeding. The term itself was coined by Darwin's cousin, Francis Galton. Galton's book *Hereditary Genius* pioneered the realm of social engineering in which human beings are viewed as mere resources to be harnessed or eliminated based upon their usefulness to the elite.

The theory of evolution is actually an atheistic approach to life and its origin. It begins with the premise that there is no God, and then seeks to explain life apart from God. Darwinism had a revolutionary impact by rejecting traditional Judeo-Christian ethics and promoting moral relativism. It played a key role in the rise of eugenicist concepts such as euthanasia, infanticide, abortion, and racial extermination.

Charles Darwin's magnum opus was first published in 1859. Most people are completely unaware that the full title was *The Origin of Species by Means of Natural Selection: The Preservation of Favoured Races in the Struggle for Life.* The Origin of the Species was and still is a eugenics manual. In 1871, Darwin's *The Descent of Man* was published. The premise of this second book by Darwin is that most people are evolutionary dead ends. Only a small elite group of people is truly evolving, and everyone else is just getting in the way and must be exterminated. This type of arrogant thinking has led to the killing of millions of people.

Adolf Hitler and the German people were avid students of Darwin's work. In fact, Darwin was Hitler's philosophical mentor. Darwinism was declared to be science and was taught in the public schools. This system of belief was the justification for killing people they considered to be inferior. The Germans were making room for an evolutionary superior race. Adolf Hitler was merely upholding a consistent ethic that rested on Darwinian foundations.

Hitler's genocide was just one of many devastating outgrowths of the Darwinian ethic.

Hitler's genocide was just one of many devastating outgrowths of the Darwinian ethic. Margaret Sanger's promotion of infanticide was another. Sanger, founder of what is now called Planned Parenthood, was an avowed and self-declared eugenicist. In 1921 she founded the American Birth Control Clinic, which later was renamed "Planned Parenthood" for marketing reasons (and in keeping with Satan's common tactic of deconstructing language). To this day, most people naively believe that Sanger was a good-hearted innovator of the family planning movement. Actually, she did more to advance the killing of people, born and unborn, in the lower socio-economic strata of American society than anyone in the twentieth century. Sanger believed that the "unfit" of society were targets to be eliminated, which included immigrants, the poor, the mentally disabled, and people of colored skin. Her collaboration with other elites in our society to advance the eugenicist agenda led to the extermination of millions of people.[1]

Satan's ultimate goal is to kill (John 10:10). He loves death and promotes death. He tried to kill Adam and Eve; he tried to kill the Messiah; and he wants to kill you. He has been killing, destroying, and devouring since he was banished from heaven. Satan "was a murderer from the beginning" (John 8:44). He thinks that his chance of winning the cosmic battle between good and evil will be much better if he can eliminate the opposition. So he does what his nature demands: he kills.

This lie is not just a force to reckon with in ages gone by. The eugenics mindset and agenda lives on in the minds of the elite to this day. Most people have no idea that famous icons in our own country, such as Bill and Melinda Gates and Oprah Winfrey, are leading eugenicists who are on record in multiple white papers and think tanks supporting and funding soft-kill and hard-kill extermination projects throughout the world that would reduce the world's population by as much as 80%![2]

Satan would have us believe that the evolution discussion is merely an intellectual issue best left for the academicians to debate in universities. But as is always the case with deception, there is much, much more to the issue than that. It is about the sanctity of life and human dignity. Which leads us to the second of Satan's top ten lies today.

Lie #2: Human life is not sacred.

A global war is raging against the sanctity of human life. Eugenics is certainly one aspect of the battle. Notable eugenicists from the past include Thomas Malthus, Charles Darwin, Francis Galton, Winston Churchill, Margaret Sanger, Theodore Roosevelt, George Bernard Shaw, and Alexander Graham Bell.

It is a mistake to think that eugenics has faded into the pages of history. The battle continues on in many different forms. The eugenics movement has some powerful people with unlimited resources at the helm, including Bill Gates, Oprah Winfrey, David Rockefeller, Ted Turner, Warren Buffet, George Soros, and Michael Bloomberg.[3] Bill Gates recently tipped off the world to the dangers of the eugenics agenda when he said, "First we got population. The world today has 6.8 billion people. That's headed up to about 9 billion. Now if we do a really great job on new vaccines, health care, reproductive health services, we lower that by perhaps 10 or 15 percent."[4]

Here we see yet another hidden agenda revealed. Notice Gates' overt reference to "vaccines." Most children in America today are routinely subjected to more than sixty-three vaccinations by the age of five. Compare that to just seven or eight vaccinations for the average child in the late 1960s and throughout the 1970s.[5] With this astounding proliferation in immunizations, one would assume that childhood illnesses would be dramatically less prominent today, if not wiped out altogether. But the statistics tell an entirely different story.

According to government statistics, the rate of autism among American children has nearly doubled over the past decade. That is not a typo. The rate of autism among American children has nearly *doubled* in less than ten years. According to a new report released by the *U.S. Centers for Disease Control and Prevention* (CDC), documented cases of autism have jumped from about 1 in 150 children back in 2000 to about 1 in 88 children in 2008, which is the last time official estimates were calculated. However, it should come as no surprise that the "official" data and the "actual" data are vastly different. The reality is much worse than the spin. The actual number is more like 1 in 29 children are diagnosed with autism.[6] Dr. Stanley Monteith writes, "The incidence of childhood asthma, diabetes, and autoimmune diseases has doubled during the past 20 years; Attention Deficit Disorder has tripled, Autism has increased 600%."[7]

Instances of childhood cancer have risen dramatically in recent years.

And autism is not the only anomaly. Instances of childhood cancer have risen dramatically in recent years. Diagnoses of leukemia, which is the most common childhood cancer, increased by more than 15% over the past twenty years. Diagnoses of brain cancers and other central nervous system tumors in children have risen by more than 25%. Given the amount of historical data available for childhood cancer statistical research, these numbers are astounding. Something is seriously wrong and experts are at a loss to explain the spike. Every year, about 12,400 children and teens under the age of twenty are diagnosed with cancer - that is one in every 330 children. Study after study has revealed a demonstrable link between childhood vaccinations and the rise in childhood cancer rates.[8]

The threat to human life also extends to the food that is produced for us to eat. Genetically modified foods (GMO) are now mainstream.[9] Our prepackaged food and drinks are contaminated with chemicals, such as aspartame and Bisphenol A (BPA). Amazingly, aspartame, which was originally promoted as a sugar substitute, is now a gratuitous ingredient in hundreds of everyday consumables—even those already containing sugar! There are multiple documented cases in court records of large pharmaceutical companies bribing doctors into prescribing powerful and dangerous drugs. The sickness caused by the chemicals ingested has become an epidemic.

The idea of the government taking over health care in the United States should have every citizen deeply concerned.

One final attack on the sanctity of human life deserves mention. The idea of the government taking over health care in the United States should have every citizen deeply concerned. Though couched in terms of providing universal coverage or socialized medicine, the real agenda is far darker. By design, the rationing of care leads to death panels, which will determine who receives medical care and who does not. For those who take the time to look beyond the "image" advanced by the powerful propaganda machines to the real "substance" of the government controlled health care plan, the eugenicist agenda is as plain as day. Sadly, most people today do not have the time or inclination to let the facts get in the way of their comfortable perceptions. Remember, "The whole world lies under the sway of the wicked one" (1 John 5:19).

Lie #3: Only a "conspiracy theorist" would believe that a small global elite is running the world at the behest of Satan.

To conspire means to agree in secret to do something wrong or illegal. Unfortunately, in keeping with the satanic principle of deconstructing language, the phrase *conspiracy theorist* has become a *de facto* pejorative label. For example, if someone uninformed is confronted with a set of facts that differ from his long-held perception of reality, the typical knee-jerk reaction is to dismiss the new information with an imperious wave of the hand and the accompanying declaration, "You must be one of those *conspiracy theorists!*"

A conspiracy theory is simply a postulation that two or more people have conspired to do something wrong or illegal.

But such a response reflects a decidedly non-intellectual approach to the matter. A conspiracy theory is simply a postulation that two or more people have conspired to do something wrong or illegal. This postulation may be correct, or incorrect. But the mere presence of a theory does not, in and of itself, say anything about the mental capacity of the one postulating the theory! As a matter of fact, labeling someone a *conspiracy theorist* simply because his postulation is radically different from anything one has heard before says more about the one hurling the label than it does about the one suggesting the theory.

Why not examine the facts on their own merits before resorting to name-calling? To be sure, many of the theories that circulate are based on nothing more than pure speculation. Some of it is even intentional misinformation or counter-intelligence purveyed by operatives of the global elite themselves. But does this mean we should reject every explanation that differs from traditional thinking? It is best to keep the old adage in mind, "I don't believe in conspiracy theories…except the ones that are true!"

The Bible teaches us that Satan is the, "ruler of this world" (John 12:31). And the Bible also teaches that we are heading toward a one-world government—a new world order if you will. Eventually, for a period of seven years, this new world order will be headed by the Antichrist—Satan's man of the hour. Then, after Christ returns to take the throne, the one-world government will be headed by Jesus Christ Himself, who will rule in perfect peace, righteousness, and judgment (Rev. 19:11-15).

There is nothing in the biblical record that precludes the one-world government from coming into existence prior to the Rapture of the Church. In reality, it may well be that we are living under a new world order long before the unveiling of the Antichrist and the Rapture of the Church. Why is it so hard for some to believe that Satan is working toward that goal right now? Not only does the Bible tell us this is precisely where we are headed, but the stage is being set all around us. The economic and geo-political framework is well underway to achieve Satan's desired goal of a new world order under his control.

During the present evil age (the Church Age), Satan has ratcheted up his efforts at world domination by influencing a secret cabal of interconnected, global, Luciferians who largely control the reality in which we live. This should not be a surprise in light of Ephesians 6:12, which plainly warns, "we do not wrestle against flesh and blood, but against principalities, against powers, against the rulers of the darkness of this age, against spiritual hosts of wickedness in the heavenly places." Satan is not omnipresent. Nor is he omniscient. Nor is he omnipotent. If he is going to advance his destructive agenda, he *must* use human agents on the frontlines.

> *History, not Fox News or CNN, holds the key to understanding reality.*

As we have said previously, those who do not know history are doomed to repeat it. History, not Fox News or CNN, holds the key to understanding reality. A thorough study of the last 2,000 years reveals that Satan has used a select group of elites, generation after generation, to work toward his goal of world domination. Secret societies such as the Club of Rome, the Illuminati, Free Masonry, and Skull & Bones represent an interconnected, demonically driven system through which Satan is advancing his agenda.

Let us be clear. This group of elite Luciferians is not monolithic. They do not control every last detail of world events. Just as Satan is not omnipotent, neither are his human envoys. There are power struggles, personality conflicts, competing agendas, and battle plans, which lead to many setbacks along the way. That is one reason the new world order has not been fully implemented yet. But make no mistake, for many centuries there has been a secret group of men at the upper echelons of power who yield profound influence on world affairs and who will stop at nothing to see Lucifer's agenda accomplished.

These are not your typical high-powered business types. We are not talking about the power brokers you hear about on the evening news. We are talking about avowed, Satan-worshipping, Luciferians who seldom welcome the limelight. Much like the ancient worshippers of the Canaanite god Molech, these are men who drink blood and sacrifice children in hidden corners of the world. These men are demon-possessed and operate on an entirely different plain than the average person. They are, after all, Satan's envoys. Though it is hard to imagine such horrific activities taking place in the dark corners of world power, the evidence is overwhelming that this is precisely the case.[10]

> These men are demon-possessed and operate on an entirely different plain than the average person. They are, after all, Satan's envoys.

This secret cabal of Luciferians holds sway over a much larger second-tier group of leaders who are also part of the new world order agenda. The second-tier is made up of people who are compartmentalized to greater or lesser degrees. That is, many may not be fully aware of the nature and extent of the evil being perpetrated by their Luciferian leaders. But they are nevertheless useful pawns in the new world order program. This second tier includes many household names among governmental leaders, corporate leaders, media moguls, and industry titans. These people are the public face of the global elite, though the average person is oblivious to their true allegiance.

The evidence for the existence of this global elite is indisputable. Woodrow Wilson, twenty-eighth President of the United States, acknowledged the powerful influence of the elite in his book *The New Freedom* (1913). He wrote, "Since I entered politics, I have chiefly had men's views confided to me privately. Some of the biggest men in the U.S., in the field of commerce and manufacturing, are afraid of somebody, are afraid of something. They know that there is a power somewhere so organized, so subtle, so watchful, so interlocked, so complete, so pervasive, that they had better not speak above their breath when they speak in condemnation of it."[11]

One of the more revealing exposés about the secret ruling elite ever printed is the work of Carroll Quigley, well-known American historian and professor at Georgetown University. Quigley, who died in 1977, is most famous for his magnum opus, *Tragedy and Hope*. In it, he carefully chronicles the secret plan of the elite to usher in the new world order. What is noteworthy about Quigley's work is that the higher education academy as a whole largely denies the existence of secret societies and a global elite. This, of course, is because the education system has long been under the direct control of the elite. So when Quigley blew the whistle on the elite's master plan with the publication of *Tragedy and Hope* in 1966, it gave instant credibility to those who had long insisted on the existence of such a secret cabal and their plan for a new world order.[12]

There are many secret and not-so-secret societies, groups, and/or clubs that serve as think tanks and strategy teams for implementing the marching orders of the elite. These include the Bilderberg Group, the Council on Foreign Relations, the Trilateral Commission, and the Bohemian Grove, among others. As one takes the time to research the wealth of information on these groups, the picture of the global elite quickly comes into focus.

> *The secret business conducted there shapes the lives of billions of people. This is where presidents are chosen, the geo-political landscape is altered, and wars are started.*

Take the Bohemian Grove for example. It is a 2,700-acre private, male-only resort in the redwoods of Monte Rio, California. Some of the most powerful men of the world gather there every year during a two-week span in July. U.S. Presidents, world leaders, cabinet officials, representatives of the financial sectors, industry, media, and military come and go to discuss major policy decisions. The secret business conducted there shapes the lives of billions of people. This is where presidents are chosen, the geo-political landscape is altered, and wars are started. But that is not all that takes place at Bohemian Grove.

Security is extremely tight at this remote resort, as one might expect given the high profile dignitaries that attend each year. Nevertheless, at least two reporters were able to infiltrate the club in the last 20 years, though only one was able to film some of the activities that take place. What his secret video revealed is appalling.

It was already widely known, through various leaks over the years, that these two-week meetings are fraught with homosexual debauchery, drunken revelry, and other bizarre rituals. But no one knew for sure precisely how evil the activities inside the Grove really were. One reporter was able to bypass security evidently because members of the Grove's security assumed he was a visiting male prostitute. He gained access to the infamous *Cremation of Care* ceremony that climaxes the two-week gathering. This closing ceremony involves the satanic ritual sacrifice of a child effigy (or at least it is presumed to be an effigy—the reporter was only able to get footage from a distance).[13]

Since the founding of the club in 1872, the Bohemian Grove's mascot has been an owl—a common symbol in satanic circles. A forty-foot owl statue is erected at the head of the lake in the Grove. This owl shrine is a centerpiece of the Cremation of Care ceremony. During the closing ceremony, the owl is set ablaze and the child sacrifice is placed before it, as the world leaders and other dignitaries offer up ritualistic chants in unison. The point of the ceremony is to "cremate" the conscience of those in attendance so that their moral compass (however weak it may be) will not stand in the way of fulfilling the plans for the coming year that had been agreed upon during the previous two weeks. These world leaders and dignitaries take a vow of silence exemplified by the Grove's motto: "Weaving spiders come not hither."

The Bohemian Grove is just one example among many of secret, ritualistic meetings of the elite. Any careful student of current events and the organizations that shape our world will discover that there are powerful forces working to bring in a new world order. As Christians, we had better know that the one pulling the strings is Satan.

Lie #4: CNN is liberal and Fox News is conservative.

Carroll Quigley was the first to expose the elite's agenda to create a false left/right paradigm in our country. He writes, "The argument that the two parties should represent opposed ideals and policies, one, perhaps, of the Right and the other of the Left, is a foolish idea acceptable only to the doctrinaire and academic thinkers. Instead, the two parties should be almost identical, so that the American people can 'throw the rascals out' at any election without leading to any profound or extreme shifts in policy."[14]

The idea is to give the public the impression that they can make a difference. Keep them distracted with minor battles while the elite's much broader agenda marches forward. The Democratic platform and the Republican platform are said to be on opposite sides of the political spectrum. However, the leaders at the upper echelons of both parties are really only pawns of the elite and are working together to usher in the new world order.

> *As long as the people of the United States continue to be cheerleaders for their own team (either Democrats or Republicans) it provides a stable system to continue advancing the satanic agenda behind the scenes.*

As long as the people of the United States continue to be cheerleaders for their own team (either Democrats or Republicans) it provides a stable system to continue advancing the satanic agenda behind the scenes. Though many well-intentioned individuals argue passionately for the ideals associated with one political party or another, the truth is it is a debate between Coke and Pepsi; there is not much difference when it comes to slowing down the elites' agenda.

Every few years, one party wrestles control of the White House, Congress, or Senate away from the other party, and yet nothing substantive ever changes. The economy worsens. Morality decays. Constitutional rights are swept away. And we continue to spiral ever closer to a full-fledged, globalist, one-world system.

The state-run media in the U.S., firmly in the grasp of the elite, helps to perpetuate this left/right paradigm. All outlets of the mainstream media are owned by one of three major corporations who are directly controlled by the elite. In addition, widespread documented cases exist of reporters being paid by the government to promote its propaganda. When the secret CIA-led program *Operation Mockingbird* was declassified, it exposed the hand-in-glove relationship between the elite and the media. *Operation Mockingbird* was established in the 1950s and involved a paid partnership between the U.S. government and the media to manipulate public opinion and advance various causes of the elite. It is not a coincidence that the content we view on television is called *programming*.

Make no mistake. The name may have changed, but *Operation Mockingbird* is ongoing. The news and entertainment provided to the people of the United States have an agenda. They exist to condition people into accepting the doctrines of the elite. The public is being prepared for a one-world system. Edward Bernays, the father of the modern public relations movement, exposed the agenda of the media in his famous book, *Propaganda*.

 The conscious and intelligent manipulation of the organized habits and opinions of the masses is an important element in democratic society. Those who manipulate this unseen mechanism of society constitute an invisible government, which is the true ruling power of our country. ...We are governed, our minds are molded, our tastes formed, our ideas suggested, largely by men we have never heard of. This is a logical result of the way in which our democratic society is organized. Vast numbers of human beings must cooperate in this manner if they are to live together as a smoothly functioning society. ...In almost every act of our daily lives, whether in the sphere of politics or business, in our social conduct or our ethical thinking, we are dominated by the relatively small number of persons...who understand the mental processes and social patterns of the masses. It is they who pull the wires, which control the public mind.[15]

The next time you are watching your favorite cable news program, just remember that it is never about what it is about. There is always more to the story.

Lie #5: Our government would never lie to us or do us harm.

Governments need to project the widespread belief that they are merely looking out for the best interests of the people they govern. They depend on this in order to secure their power over the people. The truth is much less innocent.

The government of the United States is no different. It is sad but true. The U.S. has a long history of abusing the rights of the people. Slavery, forced sterilizations (eugenics), and internment camps are just a handful of examples that point to the abuse of our government. To be sure, not every public servant is a part of the conspiracy; most are not. But rogue elements within the U.S. government have long held control behind the scenes at the behest of Satan's elite. Most public officials within the various layers of government are compartmentalized and have no idea who is really pulling the strings.

The U.S. has a long history of abusing the rights of the people.

Documented history reveals that the government routinely lies to the American people to manipulate them into supporting the actions of their leaders.[16] In the Gulf of Tonkin on August 2, 1964 there was an initial battle with North Vietnamese torpedo boats by U.S. forces. A second incident was reported by the National Security Agency to have happened on August 4, 1964. This second battle was the justification for going to war with the North Vietnamese. Declassified documents now reveal that this second incident never happened. It was completely staged to garner public support for entering the war. Let that sink in for a moment. Nearly 60,000 American soldiers were killed in action as part of a war that was predicated upon a lie.

Another vivid example of the deceit of our government is *Operation Northwoods*. In the early 1960s the Joint Chiefs of Staff desperately wanted to wage war with Cuba. Needing an excuse for war, they unanimously signed off on the plan code named *Operation Northwoods*. The strategy was diabolical:

- innocent Americans would be shot on the streets of the United States
- terrorist attacks would be staged in Washington D.C., Miami, and other strategic places with innocent people being framed for bombings
- planes would be hijacked
- refugee boats fleeing Cuba would be sunk
- it was suggested a U.S. ship could be blown up in Guantanamo Bay so it could be blamed on Cuba

All of this would give the military the cover they needed to launch a war against Cuba. Although this particular plot was never carried out, it does illustrate perfectly the willingness of our government to manipulate the people of the United States. American history is rife with examples of similar plans that were in fact carried out at home and abroad.

In the art of war, these types of actions are referred to as *false flag operations*. Governments have a longstanding tradition of using this tactic. The term *false flag operation* originally came from the concept of naval vessels flying another country's flag to deceive and confuse other ships. It is now used in military parlance whenever a government stages its own attack but blames other countries, or terrorist groups, for the attack in order to influence public opinion, advance an agenda, or to lead the nation to war. This powerful tool is used to control the people governed because it provides officials with the excuse that they are simply defending the country from the aggression of outside forces.

When the Luciferians need to advance their cause by expanding their borders or increasing their power, false flag operations can be a very effective strategy.

When the Luciferians need to advance their cause by expanding their borders or increasing their power, false flag operations can be a very effective strategy. A typical three-step process would look something like this: (1) Fabricate or provoke an enemy. (2)

Stage an attack from that enemy. (3) Retaliate in response to the "attack." The public hastily and enthusiastically lines up in support and will allow almost any infringement on their rights in order to defeat this new "enemy."

A related military technique is called *stand down*. The stand down technique has been part of military strategy for centuries and is routinely taught in military training schools. Dr. Steve R. Pieczenik, former U.S. Navy Captain, served as the Deputy Assistant Secretary of State under three different administrations (Nixon, Ford, and Carter). He later worked under Reagan and Bush senior. Pieczenik currently works as a consultant for the Department of Defense. He achieved two prestigious Harry C. Solomon Awards at the Harvard Medical School while at the same time completing his Ph.D. at MIT. To say the least, Pieczenik is a respected, top government insider. He states unequivocally, "I taught stand down and false flag operations at the national war college. I've taught it with all my operatives."[17]

So what is a stand down operation? In this scenario, the government becomes aware of an impending attack, or in some cases provokes an attack, but intentionally does nothing in order to justify a retaliatory strike. Serious and extensive research into the events of September 11, 2001 have led many experts to conclude that this is precisely what happened that terrible day.

There is much more than meets the eye when it comes to the world-changing events of 9-11.

At face value, the idea that an inept band of nineteen carousing men, under the leadership of a wealthy dialysis patient hiding in a cave in Afghanistan, was able to bring the mightiest military in the history of the world to its knees for two hours, without any support from the inside, is dubious at best. There is much more than meets the eye when it comes to the world-changing events of 9-11. Thousands of architects, engineers, pilots, scientists, educators, theologians, first responders, eyewitnesses, insiders, high-level government officials, and scholars are on record stating that the official story is false. Moreover, six of the ten 9-11 Commissioners responsible for investigating 9-11 and producing the official *9-11 Commission Report* now believe that certain elements of the U.S. Government were somehow complicit in the attacks.

But all of this is beyond the scope of this book. What is important to notice is that given the pivotal role that the 9-11 events played in reshaping American society, and indeed the world, it is not hard to imagine how the false flag/stand down concept may very well have played a role.[18] Such a possibility may be difficult for most people to fathom, but remember the words of Hitler, "The bigger the lie the easier it is to pull it off."

One recent example of an admitted false flag operation is the so-called underwear bomber. On December 25, 2009 Umar Farouk Abdulmutallab allegedly tried to blow up Northwest Airlines flight 253 by hiding a bomb in his underwear. This incident became the basis for two key developments in the procedures of the TSA at airport security stations. First, it provided justification to roll out the body scanners at airports throughout the country. Second, it provided justification for TSA agents to stick their hands inside the pants of those travelers who opted out of the body scanners, to ensure that they were not hiding bombs.

Most Americans continue to accept this initial story about "the underwear bomber" even though subsequent hearings before Congress and court proceedings have exposed the entire incident as a manufactured event. But the true story does not advance the elite's agenda of a police state, so it got little attention in the mainstream news.

It eventually came out, on record, that Abdulmutallab was a CIA patsy who was escorted on the plane by a State Department official (the famous "sharp-dressed man" that witnesses on the plane described leading Abdulmutallab to his seat prior to take-off). Evidently, the goal was to stage an attack and influence public opinion about airline security. Kurt Haskell, an attorney and eyewitness of the events on the plane and in the airport prior to take-off, testified at Abdulmutallab's trial and blew the lid off this false flag operation—

fingering the State Department agent who got Abdulmutallab on the plane.[19]

It has also come out that Michael Chertoff, former head of Homeland Security, personally profited from the rollout of the body scanners throughout America. His company, *The Chertoff Group*, was a security consultant to the primary manufacturer of the machines and Chertoff himself was pushing the implementation of these machines. All that was needed was an unfreezing event to justify the mandatory placement of them in U.S. airports.

> *The romanticized notion that American government leaders are somehow immune to the depravity of man and would never do us harm is naïve.*

Christians would do well to remember that governments are made up of people who sin. The romanticized notion that American government leaders are somehow immune to the depravity of man and would never do us harm is naïve. Those who are not redeemed by Christ are now walking, "according to the course of this world, according to the prince of the power of the air, the spirit who now works in the sons of disobedience" (Eph. 2:2). And they are capable of the same kind of atrocities that other world leaders have perpetrated throughout human history.

Lie #6: Global warming is a problem, and man is the cause of it.

The Hegelian Dialectic is a framework that is used to guide the thoughts and actions of people into a problem with a goal of implementing a predetermined solution. It starts with a public policy that the ruling elite want to establish. In order to help establish it, a problem is created, while anticipating the reaction of the people to the given crisis. The population is thus conditioned that change is needed and the solution is then presented, which is the public policy or agenda that the elite intended to accomplish all along.

A prime example of the use of the Hegelian Dialectic to advance the elite's agenda is the issue of global warming. It is a manufactured problem intended to lead to an ultimate goal. One of the solutions that came out of the alleged global warming "problem" is a global carbon tax. This, in turn, must be enforced at a global level, which leads us to the elite's real agenda, a global government.

In 2009 global warming was exposed for the hoax that it is. E-mails from a global research center in the United Kingdom revealed scientists deleting and altering data to hide the truth that global temperatures have actually been cooling. The scientists at the University of East Anglia's Climate Research Unit were caught manipulating data to support their cause. Additional internal memos exposed the whole global warming "crisis" as a scam from the start. There never was a problem. It was a manufactured crisis to achieve a particular end; namely, the imposition of taxes to bankrupt citizens and bring more money to the elite.

> *The average person does not have the desire to search for the truth. It is much easier to accept the propaganda and lies that are being spoon-fed to the public.*

Yet amazingly, despite being exposed as a fraud, the global warming hoax lives on, aided and abetted by the mainstream media. It is as if the scandal never happened! I am amazed at the number of people I come across in my travels who are completely unaware of the now infamous *Copenhagen Documents* that exposed the global warming hoax. Once again, Satan's deception has gotten easier and easier. The average person does not have the desire to search for the truth. It is much easier to accept the propaganda and lies that are being spoon-fed to the public.

Even if the hoax had not been exposed, the student of Scripture should recognize that global warming cannot be true. Genesis 8:22 teaches, "While the earth remains, seedtime and harvest, cold and heat, winter and summer, and day and night shall not cease." We have the promise from the Creator that as long as the earth remains there will be both cold and heat, winter and summer.

The widespread acceptance of the global warming hoax has led many people to exchange, "the truth of God for the lie" (Rom. 1:25). They are worshipping and serving the creation rather than the Creator. The public schools systems and universities have been an avenue for spreading this lie.

Lie #7: Compulsory government schooling is the only way to educate our children.

Another key weapon in the elite's arsenal is the conditioning of children. The earlier you capture the mind, the easier it becomes to control the person. Those who take the time to study the history of compulsory government schooling in America will discover that this was precisely the goal from the start. It was never about helping children learn. Those who foisted compulsory government schooling upon American children had a much more sinister motive.

That is not to say, of course, that every public school teacher or administrator is part of the ultimate conspiracy. Like all of the elite's plans, compartmentalization is key. Only those in the upper echelons of the U.S. Department of Education, the textbook industry, and related entities are aware of the real agenda behind compulsory government schooling. The seminal work exposing compulsory schooling as part of a broader, nefarious conspiracy is by Charlotte Iserbyt.

Iserbyt is a highly respected leader who served in the Department of Education during the Reagan Administration. She was fired when she blew the whistle after uncovering powerful evidence of the elite's compulsory schooling agenda. Her work, *The Deliberate Dumbing Down of America*, is a must-read for those who are interested in the truth behind the compulsory government schooling movement in our country.

It is assumed by a great number of people that mandatory government schooling is vastly superior to any alternative. It is for this reason that we see in many countries (Brazil, Sweden, Germany,

Georgia, Greece, Iceland, Ukraine, etc.) homeschooling has been made illegal. An even larger number of countries technically allow it, but restrict it out of existence by regulation. Many U.S. states have similar regulations. But is government schooling the only approach to educating our children?

> *Any student of history should recognize that public schools have been, and continue to be, a place of indoctrination - for good or for bad.*

Most people are unaware that it was not until 1918 that every state in the Union had laws mandating compulsory schooling. Any student of history should recognize that public schools have been, and continue to be, a place of indoctrination—for good or for bad.[20] We must remember that there is a difference between educating children and schooling them. Open-source learning worked fine for 5,850 years of human history. And it works fine today.

Lie #8: The battle can be won at the ballot box.

> *Ultimately, a democracy amounts to two wolves and a sheep voting on what is for dinner. The majority does not always act in the best interest of society.*

Is America a democracy? Most people assume so. But the knowledgeable student of U.S. history knows that our country was founded as a republic, not a democracy. The democratic process plays a role in our system of government, but it does not (or should not) define us. Ultimately, a democracy amounts to two wolves and a sheep voting on what is for dinner. The majority does not always act in the best interest of society.

For example, if 90% of Americans voted for forced abortions to advance the elite's agenda of depopulation, would that make it acceptable? Of course not. Always be leery of governance by majority vote. It sounds appealing, but it can come back to bite you.

The U.S. Declaration of Independence affirms that our citizens are endowed with certain unalienable rights. *Unalienable* refers to rights that cannot be given or taken away. They are ours by virtue of being human beings. They are given by God Himself. The elite have long targeted these unalienable rights bestowed by our Creator because they stand in the way of the elite's agenda.

> *Satan's elite figured out long ago that democracies are easy to manipulate.*

Satan's elite figured out long ago that democracies are easy to manipulate. Using the Hegelian Dialectic discussed in lie #6 above, the hidden agenda of the Luciferians can be promoted through the ballot box. They actually get the public to vote in favor of policies and laws that undermine our natural rights as human beings. Their approach is, "Let's get the lowly plebs to want what we want them to want, then give it to them!"

If the elite cannot get the public to dutifully go along with their own demise, they will manipulate the vote to serve their ends. Voter fraud is as old as the democratic process itself. As long as human beings are involved, you can count on some degree of fraud. Joseph Stalin famously declared, "Those who cast the votes decide nothing; those who count the votes decide everything." The elite have used their power, connections, and leverage to bring voter fraud to a whole new level in the twenty-first century.

Many well-intentioned, patriotic Americans, still believe that we can overcome any evil agenda—no matter how widespread or powerful—by voting our way out of the problem. Such idealism reflects an optimistic view of the good of mankind. But it is woefully naïve. In most instances, the ballot box holds no hope for overcoming the satanic agenda. In fact, the actual "ballot box" does not even exist anymore.

Across the globe, but especially in the United States, electronic voting machines have become the tool of choice for ensuring the desired outcome in an election. Defying written election laws in county after county, officials have outsourced the collection, tabulation, and reporting of voting results to privately owned corporations not realizing that these very corporations, such as Diebold, are under the control of the elite. There is little or no chain of custody ensuring the validity of the votes.

With digital technology, an operative sitting in a small office in Cleveland can literally change the outcome of the Presidential vote in Michigan with a few clicks of the mouse, and no one ever knows. The days of certifying written ballots and keeping them under the watchful eye of elected local officials are long gone.[21]

To be sure, there are still places in America where the democratic process remains pure (small districts, local communities, etc.). But by and large the democratic process has been hijacked by the elite. Those who take the time to research this subject will awaken to an entirely new reality when it comes to American politics.

Lie #9: The U.S. Government prints its own money.

Thomas Jefferson sounded a somber warning when he stated, "I believe that banking institutions are more dangerous to our liberties than standing armies." Are you aware that a handful of families from within the satanic elite privately own the Federal Reserve? The Fed is a private, offshore, central bank. The Federal Reserve is no more "federal" than *Federal Express*. It is a privately owned, for-profit entity. In a secret meeting in 1910 on Jekyll Island (an island off the coast of the U.S. state of Georgia), members of the elite met to devise a plot for the pilfering of America.

Woodrow Wilson was elected President in 1912 based largely on the support of these elite "banksters." In exchange, he had agreed to support the Federal Reserve Act. After his election, on December 23, 1913, President Wilson signed the bill into law. Our country would never be the same. This Act transferred control of the money supply of the United States from Congress (as required by the U.S. Constitution) to the private global elite.

Years later, Woodrow Wilson would lament, "I am a most unhappy man. I have unwittingly ruined my country. A great industrial nation is now controlled by its system of credit. We are no longer a government by free opinion, no longer a government by conviction and the vote of the majority, but a government by the opinion and duress of a small group of dominant men."

> We are no longer a government by free opinion, no longer a government by conviction and the vote of the majority, but a government by the opinion and duress of a small group of dominant men.

So who owns the FED today? The Rothschilds of London and Berlin; Lazard Brothers of Paris; Israel Moses Seif of Italy; Kuhn, Loeb and Warburg of Germany; and the Lehman Brothers, Goldman, Sachs and the Rockefeller families of New York.[22]

How does the U.S. monetary system work? To begin, we need to recognize that the Federal Reserve does not print money. The actual printing presses are operated by the Department of Treasury. The Federal Reserve controls the money supply by placing an order with the U.S. Bureau of Engraving and Printing. What is printed—what we call "currency"—is actually Federal Reserve *Notes*. If you look carefully at any piece of U.S. paper currency, it clearly states that it is a "note." These notes are distributed to Federal Reserve Banks, who in turn sell them at face value to commercial banks. The private owners of the Federal Reserve continue to get richer and richer the more notes they sell! Is there any wonder why the printing presses never seem to slow down?

> The Reserve Notes that we use are not "money," in the historic use of the term.

What does it mean that the bills we use are Federal Reserve Notes? The Reserve Notes that we use are not "money," in the historic use of the term. Throughout the history of civilization, "money" has referred to a designated means of exchange that has an *inherent value*. Before 1971 Federal Reserve Notes were backed by an equivalent amount of gold held by the U.S. Treasury, giving them inherent value. Under

President Nixon the gold standard was abandoned, which created a fiat currency.

This means that Federal Reserve Notes are no longer backed by gold. Federal Reserve Notes are now created out of nothing—by the decree of the Federal Reserve. They are backed only by the declaration of the United States government that this is legal tender. As more Reserve Notes are printed they become worth less in value, leading to inflation. As prices skyrocket because of inflation, people turn to debt. Every fiat currency in history has eventually collapsed, and this one will too.

It only costs a few cents to create these Reserve Notes. The American people are then billed for the full face value of the notes. To make matters worse, we are charged interest to borrow what they are calling money. Not only is this unconstitutional (Article I, Section 8, Clause 5 and Article I, Section 10, Clause 1), but it is also a complete fraud. This is all by design. The Luciferian elite know exactly what they are doing. In order to usher in the new world order, they must first bankrupt every major economy—a goal that is very near to being accomplished.[23]

Lie #10: Big Brother is just a television show.

The United States can no longer truthfully be referred to as the land of the free. To some, that statement will sound unpatriotic. But it is not unpatriotic to acknowledge reality. And it is not inconsistent to love the principles of freedom on which our country was founded, while at the same time recognize that the global elite long ago hijacked our government.

In many ways, the "land of the free, home of the brave" has become the "land of the slave, home of the coward."

In many ways, the "land of the free, home of the brave" has become the "land of the slave, home of the coward." One can scarcely think of any area of our lives that the government does not monitor or seek to control. Cities are now blanketed with surveillance cameras. East Orange, New Jersey, for example, has recently joined a growing list of cities that have taken surveillance to a new level. As citizens are monitored by thousands of cameras, a red beam of light shines down on people from streetlights if it is suspected by officials that they are about to commit a crime. The police want them to know they are being watched. Law enforcement will intervene before a crime even takes place. This sort of pre-crime technology is all the rave at law enforcement conferences, technology trade shows, and security expos.

Most major cities in the U.S. now use traffic light cameras, and in some cases speeding cameras, to track you as you drive. The popular CBS television show *Person of Interest* actually uses real surveillance footage from cameras all over New York City as part of every episode. This show is one of the more blatant examples of elite propaganda on television today. It conditions us to be comfortable being watched 24/7.

A growing number of municipalities have implemented a system of immediate fund withdrawals for speeding and traffic light violations. Using the same technology that passive toll road systems use, where money is automatically debited from your checking account or charged to your credit card when you pass through a toll booth, cities are automatically taking your money when big brother catches you allegedly speeding or running a red light. These cameras are far from perfect and study after study has shown them to be ineffective and even counterproductive in making the roads safer. Nevertheless, the government remains undaunted and proceeds with imposing sentence without trial, judge, or jury.

All across the country, regional, federally funded Threat Fusion Centers have been set up to monitor and synthesize data on citizens. Law enforcement officials then avail themselves of the data at these centers to spy on citizens whom they think look suspicious. These Threat Fusion Centers are part of a larger plan to prepare for civil unrest once the government declares martial law and activates dozens of FEMA camps throughout the country. Given the precarious state of the economy and the dangerous geo-political climate that has been created by design by the elite, we may be facing such a scenario sooner than we think. I realize this sounds like something right out of Orwell's *1984*. But if you take the time to do the research, you will discover it is not fiction but reality.[24]

In Texas, random checkpoints have been established all over the state. At these checkpoints, all drivers must stop, get out, show their papers, and allow their car to be searched—without probable cause or warrant. It is standard procedure. Even worse, Texas has adopted "no refusal blood-draws." This means that if you are suspected of drunk driving you will have a needle forcibly stuck in your arm and have blood drawn for testing. And pending legislation means that soon this will be done, not back at the police station, but right on the side of the road!

I know what some of you are thinking. "Those dangerous drunk drivers deserve what they get!" But remember…we are not talking about people who have been convicted in a court of law by a jury of their peers. We are talking about *anyone* who gets pulled over for *suspicion* of drunk driving? Who determines whether you look *suspicious*? The police officer on the spot, by decree, can unilaterally decide to forcibly take your blood. What about our rights against self-incrimination and warrantless searches? Imagine the upstanding citizen whose vehicle momentarily drifts over the line on a windy day on the Interstate. "Pull over. Roll up your sleeve." It is already happening.

> *The government is using presidential directives and congressional acts to contravene the Constitution at every turn.*

The government is using presidential directives and congressional acts to contravene the Constitution at every turn. The most recent version of the National Defense Authorization Act (NDAA) allows the U.S. President to declare any American Citizen to be a "terrorist," and then direct the U.S. military, CIA, FBI or any other law enforcement agency to hunt down the individual and kill him—no arrest, no trial, no judge, no jury. If you are labeled a "terrorist," you can and will be killed. This is precisely what happened with American citizen Anwar al-Awlaki. To be clear, I am not suggesting that al-Awlaki was a good man. By all accounts it appears that he was not. But should the President have the right to order the assassination of every citizen he thinks is a "bad man" without a trial?

Americans have become shocked to learn that most of our communications (over the internet, cell phones and land lines) are not as secure as we would like to believe. Corporations, including AT&T, Verizon, and Google, are all too willing to hand over their customers' sensitive data to the government.[25] Students in Philadelphia's Lower Merion School District and several other school districts across the country learned the dangers of our time when school administrators were caught spying on students at home through the webcams on school issued laptops.

In the name of security from a manufactured enemy, Americans have voluntarily surrendered our freedoms. Each year millions of Americans line up to go through naked body scanners at airports. Literally hundreds of independent, scientific studies by institutions such as John's Hopkins, Columbia University, and the University of California have shown that these machines pose a grave health risk. Transportation Security Administration (TSA) agents at Logan International Airport in Boston, Massachusetts (the first airport to implement the naked body scanners) are involved in a law suit against the manufacturer of the scanners because workers at that airport have been diagnosed with cancer at a rate that is eight times the national average.[26]

Yet, even if the machines were not a serious threat to the lives of Americans, they violate our 4th Amendment right against warrantless searches. Notwithstanding denials by TSA officials, the pornographic images captured by these machines are being saved on the machines' hard drives. Federal officials are on record admitting this fact.[27] Moreover, internal memos from the TSA state that the TSA requires all airport body scanners it purchases to be able to store and transmit images for testing, training, and evaluation purposes. The user's manuals from the top two manufacturers of the naked body scanners

Remember... almost everything you hear in the mainstream news is a lie.

also are clear that images are saved by default on the hard drives unless this feature is manually disabled.

Remember... almost everything you hear in the mainstream news is a lie. So when you hear DHS Secretary Janet Napolitano or TSA Administrator John Pistole deny that images are being saved, do not believe it. It is hard to say whether they are intentionally "deceiving" or "being deceived" themselves by someone higher up (2 Tim. 3:13). But there is no question that what they are saying is not true. Ten minutes of research will yield literally hundreds of official, declassified and/ or leaked documents proving that images are in fact being saved and that the radiation emitted by these machines is extremely harmful, especially to children.

For those who refuse to be radiated by the naked body scanners, an invasive grope-down awaits. The "enhanced pat down" as it is called (notice the example of deconstructing language) is conditioning citizens to allow officials to touch us in places previously off limits. Not only does the TSA search inside citizens' pants, but now the long arm of the TSA extends beyond airports to conduct their searches on trains, subways, ferry terminals, sporting events, public schools, and highway checkpoints. The most recent statistics show that there are more TSA agents working outside of airports than inside. The elite know that many local law enforcement officers will eventually wise up to what is going on and will refuse to violate their oath to uphold the Constitution. That is why they are assembling a massive army of civilian agents (the TSA).

One final attack on our liberties deserves mention. Part of the scheme to usher in the new world order necessarily involves the disarming of American citizens. The founders of our country envisioned the real possibility that future rogue elements within the government may try to attack us and do us harm. That is why the Constitution guarantees citizens the right to keep and bear arms—so that citizens can protect themselves from *the government*. Thomas

Thomas Jefferson astutely observed, "The beauty of the Second Amendment is that it will not be needed until they try to take it."

Jefferson astutely observed, "The beauty of the Second Amendment is that it will not be needed until they try to take it." The Luciferian agenda has been slowly undermining the Second Amendment for many decades. But the attack on our right to bear arms has moved into full throttle in the last few years. The military and local law enforcement agencies are working in tandem doing gun confiscation drills all over the country. A simple web search for "gun confiscation drills" will yield hundreds of reports.[28]

Big Brother is not just a television show. Establishing a police state is a key component in the elites' plan for creating a new world order. Thomas Jefferson prophetically warned, "Those who surrender freedom for security will not have, nor do they deserve, either one."

The Remedy

We are approaching the time when the words of the Apostle Paul will come true, "For when they say, 'Peace and safety!' then sudden destruction comes upon them, as labor pains upon a pregnant woman. And they shall not escape" (1 Thess. 5:3). This is the perfect reminder that as we approach the end times the people of the world will be proclaiming a message that is vastly different from the truth. As we awaken to the truth we become better prepared to live for Jesus Christ during these last days.

In the next chapter we will look at the remedy for deception. No matter how overwhelming Satan's deception may seem, always remember that the smallest amount of light will dispel the darkness. Knowledge is power. Satan's scheme is ultimately a battle for the mind. It is an information war. The more we know the truth, the harder it is for him to deceive. In the next chapter we will look at how to respond to deception.

Discussion Questions – Chapter 8

1. Describe the impact Darwin had on the world?

2. Who was Margaret Sanger?

3. What is eugenics?

4. Describe the Hegelian Dialectic.

5. What is a *false flag* operation?

6. What is a *stand down* operation?

7. What are unalienable rights?

8. Who owns the Federal Reserve Bank?

9. What are some ways the government is implementing a police state today?

Endnotes - Chapter 8

1. One of the more powerful "smoking guns" revealing the true agenda of Planned Parenthood from its inception is the infamous Planned Parenthood Memorandum on Population Control. A copy is available here http://static. infowars.com/2011/12/i/article-images/jaffememo-watersterilants.pdf.

2. One example of a soft-kill technique in the Luciferians' agenda is the contamination of drinking water supplies with fluoride and other toxic waste products. See *The Case Against Fluoride: How Hazardous Waste Ended Up in Our Drinking Water and the Bad Science and Powerful Politics That Keep It There.*

3. For more information see http://theintelhub.com/2011/05/08/billionaires-for-eugenics/.

4. Paul Joseph Watson, "Bill Gates: Use Vaccines to Lower Population," http://www.infowars.com/bill-gates-use-vaccines-to-lower-population/ (accessed March 18, 2012).

5. See http://www.sayingnotovaccines.com/ and http://www.infowars.com/vaccination-myths-and-truths/

6. See http://vaxtruth.org/2012/04/when-1-in-88-is-really-1-in-29/

7. http://imva.info/index.php/vaccines/childhood-immunization/

8. For more information on the dangers of vaccinations see http://www.russellblaylockmd.com/ and http://vaccinesafetyfirst.com/Home.html and *Callous Disregard* by Andrew J. Wakefield.

9. For more information see http://www.nongmoproject.org/

10. There are many excellent resources detailing the history, structure, and identity of Satan's global elite. A simple web search will reveal enough data to keep the researcher busy for months. A few resources stand out. *Brotherhood of Darkness* by Dr. Stanley Monteith; *Bloodlines of the Illuminati* by Fritz Springmeier; *The Naked Capitalist* by Cleon Skousen; *Tragedy and Hope* by Carroll Quigley; *The Demonic Roots of Globalism* by Gary Kah; *America's Secret Establishment: An Introduction to the Order of Skull & Bones* by Antony C. Sutton; *Rule By Secrecy* by Jim Maars; *None Dare Call It Conspiracy* by Gary Allen; *Superclass* by David Rothkopf. *The Rise of the Fourth Reich: The Secret Societies That Threaten To Take Over America* by Jim Marrs.

11. Woodrow Wilson, *The New Freedom*.

12. For an excellent summary of Quigley's book see *The Naked Capitalist* by W. Cleon Skousen or *None Dare Call It Conspiracy* by Gary Allen.

13. See the video, *Dark Secrets Inside Bohemian Grove* available at www.infowars. com and elsewhere.

14. Carroll Quigley, *Tragedy and Hope*.

15. Edward Bernays, *Propaganda*.

16. See Judge Andrew P. Napolitano, *Lies the Government Told you*; Jesse Venture and Dick Russell, *63 Documents the Government Doesn't Want You to Read*.

17. See http://www.infowars.com/911-a-time-for-truth/; http://www.prisonplanet.com/top-us-government-insider-bin-laden-died-in-2001-911-a-false-flag.html; http://www.infowars.com/dr-steve-pieczenik-america-is-held-hostage-by-the-military-industrial-complex/.

18. For more information about the 9-11 attacks see David Ray Griffin, *The New Pearl Harbor Revisited: 9/11, the Cover-Up, and the Exposé*; Webster Griffin Tarpley, *9/11 Synthetic Terror: Made in USA, Fifth Edition*; and many other scholarly works by David Ray Griffin, theologian, and leading scholarly 9/11 researcher.

19. See http://www.infowars.com/breaking-kurt-haskell-exposes-government-false-flag-operation-during-underwear-bomber-sentencing/

20. For more information about compulsory government schooling, see the film *IndoctriNation* available at http://indoctrinationmovie.com. See also the following resources: *Weapons of Mass Instruction* by John Taylor Gatto; *The Underground History of American Education* by John Taylor Gatto; *The Deliberate Dumbing Down of America* by Charlotte Iserbyt; *None Dare Call It Education* by John A. Stormer; *Public Schools, Public Menace: How Public Schools Lie To Parents and Betray Our Children* by Joel Turtel; *Walking Targets: How Our Psychologized Classrooms Are Producing a Nation of Sitting Ducks* by B.K. Eakman.

21. For a stunning, well-researched documentary on electronic voting machines see the film *Votergate*. See also http://www.blackboxvoting.org/.

22. http://www.globalresearch.ca/index.php?context=va&aid=10489.

23. The preeminent, scholarly work on the history of the Federal Reserve is *The Creature from Jekyll Island* by G. Edward Griffin.

24. http://m.wired.com/threatlevel/2012/03/ff_nsadatacenter/all/1; http://www.infowars.com/the-72-threat-fusion-centers-were-designed-to-threaten-you/.

25. For more information see *Shadow Government* by Grant Jeffrey and the NY Times bestseller, *The End of America: Letter of Warning to a Young Patriot* by Naomi Wolf; *Big Brother: The Orwellian Nightmare Come True* by Mark Dice; *Spychips: How Major Corporations and Government Plan to Track Your Every Purchase and Watch Your Every Move* by Katherine Albrecht and Liz McIntyre. See also: http://m.wired.com/threatlevel/2012/03/ff_nsadatacenter/all/1.

26. There are literally thousands of articles from the past several years detailing the dangers of the naked body scanners. But if you get your news solely from CNN or Fox News, you may have missed them. Here is just a sampling: http://articles.sun-sentinel.com/2011-12-25/news/fl-tsa-scanner-concern-20111223_1_body-scanners-backscatter-machines-millimeter-wave-scanners; http://travel.usatoday.com/flights/post/2010/07/full-body-scanners-pose-cancer-risk-at-airports-us-scientists-warn/98552/1; http://www.infowars.com/cancer-surges-in-body-scanner-operators-tsa-launches-cover-up/; http://epic.org/privacy/backscatter/radiation_hopkins.pdf; http://www.prisonplanet.com/columbia-university-body-scanners-increase-risk-of-skin-cancer.html; http://stoptsascanners.blogspot.com/2011/05/scientists-letter-to-john-holdren.html; http://www.bloomberg.com/apps/news?pid=newsarchive&sid=aoG.YbbvnkzU&pos=11; http://epic.org/privacy/backscatter/radiation_NIST.pdf; http://www.infowars.com/full-body-scanners-increase-cancer-risk/.
27. http://news.cnet.com/8301-31921_3-20012583-281.html
28. For example: http://www.prisonplanet.com/new-york-national-guard-units-scan-vehicles-for-gun-confiscations.html; http://publicintelligence.net/vigilant-guard-2010-riot-control-detention-drills/; http://www.carrollspaper.com/main.asp?SectionID=1&SubSectionID=1&ArticleID=7451&TM=55111.9; http://www.infowars.com/photos-u-s-army-domestic-quick-reaction-force-riot-control-training/.

Chapter 9

Responding to Deception

Therefore let us not sleep, as others do, but let us watch and be sober. - 1 Thessalonians 5:6

Rick Rescorla is the name of a true American hero. He has become known as the man who predicted the events of September 11, 2001. More importantly, he is responsible for saving thousands of lives.

Morgan Stanley was the largest tenant in the World Trade Center, and as the Vice President of Security, Rescorla had a formidable job to do. He took his responsibility seriously, and in 1992 he warned the Port Authority that the World Trade Center could easily be attacked by placing a truck bomb in the basement parking garage. When his prediction came true in 1993, Rescorla guided people to safety and was the last man out of his building.

His vigilance to security had him concerned about the future. Rescorla firmly believed that the World Trade Center would be the center of another attack. He even believed that the next event could be a plane crashing into one of the towers. The Vice President of Security recommended that Morgan Stanley should leave Manhattan, but the company had a lease until the end of 2006.

If Morgan Stanley was going to remain in the World Trade Center, then Rescorla needed a plan. Long before the events of 2001, he came up with an evacuation strategy. All company officials and employees were forced to practice evacuating the buildings every three months. With offices high up in the South Tower, an attack on this building would put them in a precarious position. The practice drills were massively unpopular with the staff at Morgan Stanley. Some of the people thought Rescorla was completely out of his mind.

American Airlines Flight 11 hit Tower 1 of the Trade Center at 8:46 a.m. The official response by the building officials in Tower 2 was remarkable. The building speaker system began to repeat the message that people should remain in their offices. The employees of Morgan Stanley knew better because they had been prepared for this specific catastrophe. Ignoring the message to stay in the building, Rescorla put his plan into action.

The orderly evacuation, of 2,700 employees from roughly 20 floors of World Trade Center 2 and 1,000 from World Trade Center 5, worked like clockwork. The Vice President of Security even sang to the people over a bullhorn to keep them calm as they made their exit. Most of Morgan Stanley's employees were out of the building when United Airlines Flight 175 hit Tower 2 at 9:03 a.m. Rescorla then returned to the building to rescue others still inside. He was last seen heading up the stairs of the 10th floor of Tower 2 shortly before the building exploded. His remains have never been recovered.

Because of his heroic actions, only a handful of Morgan Stanley's 2,700 employees from Tower 2 died on that horrible day. Rick Rescorla gave his life so that others might live.

The surviving employees of Morgan Stanley have a new perspective about their former Vice President of Security. Those unpopular evacuation drills and preparations had saved their lives. History has demonstrated that Rescorla was no fool. He was a man that was ready for the worst. Rescorla was prepared for the day most people thought would never come.

We can either prepare, or be lured into complacency.

The question that confronts us is whether or not we are prepared for the events that are about to unfold in our time. We cannot know the specifics of what lies ahead, or the timing of the return of our Lord for His Church, but we can know from the Word of God that deception and global control will continue to increase. We can either prepare, or be lured into complacency. "A prudent person foresees danger and takes precautions. The simpleton goes blindly on and suffers the consequences" (Prov. 22:3, NLT). In the Apostle Paul's second epistle to the church at Thessalonica we find helpful instruction on how to ready ourselves for the days ahead.

Do Not Fear

The reason the Christians at Thessalonica were plagued by fear was because they had been led astray about the return of the Lord. This robbed these precious believers of the blessed hope that we have in Jesus Christ. The church was, "not to be soon shaken in mind or troubled" (2 Thess. 2:2).

When you first wake up to the reality and severity of Satan's deception, it is easy to become paralyzed by fear. Thankfully, Christians do not need to fear the worst of the worst. Even though it may look like it at times, we are not in the Day of the Lord! As we witnessed earlier (see chapter 5), the Rapture of the Church will take place before the Tribulation unfolds. This is the teaching of 2 Thessalonians 2:3-4. The Church of Jesus Christ will be gone when the Antichrist dominates the world.

The danger with fear is that it makes us susceptible to deception. Think of when you are home alone late at night. As you hear an unfamiliar noise, fear begins to creep into your mind. Before long you are tricked into thinking the absolute worst, "Is someone in your home, out to get you?" Fear weakens our mental defenses.

The power of fear is illustrated for us perfectly in the Word of God. Galatians 2:1-10 reveals that the Apostle Paul went with Barnabas and Titus to meet with the leaders of the church at Jerusalem. The topic at hand could not have been more important. The discussion centered on the Gospel of Christ and the work of Paul amongst the Gentiles. It was agreed that the same gospel message should be preached to both Jews and Gentiles. There is no need for Gentiles to keep the Jewish law in order to be eternally saved. It is important to note that the Apostle Peter (Cephas) was a part of this meeting (Gal. 2:9).

Antioch had become a strategic center for reaching the Gentile world with the Gospel of Christ. The Apostle Paul informs us of the situation, "Now when Peter had come to Antioch, I withstood him to his face, because he was to be blamed; for before certain men came from James, he would eat with the Gentiles; but when they came, he withdrew and separated himself, fearing those who were of the circumcision" (Gal. 2:11-12). At Antioch Jewish and Gentile Christians ate together in regular fellowship.

This should not have been a problem for Peter. He had already directly wrestled with this issue himself, before the events at Antioch (Acts 10:9-15). He even had stated at one time, "You know how unlawful it is for a Jewish man to keep company with or go to one of another nation. But God has shown me that I should not call any man common or unclean" (Acts 10:28).

When certain Jewish men came to Antioch, the Jewish Christians retreated and began to separate themselves from the Gentile believers. Peter caved and followed the Jewish Christians into this hypocrisy. The reason for his actions was clear, "he withdrew and separated himself, fearing those who were of the circumcision" (Gal. 2:12). Fear is a powerful motivator, and it opens the door to compromise.

It seems quite natural to have fears. But should we? In the same Pauline letter where we are warned that things will get "worse and worse," we also are reminded, "God has not given us a spirit of fear, but of power and of love and of a sound mind" (2 Tim. 1:7). The Spirit of God empowers believers to serve Christ, not to live in fear. Simply stated, fear is not of God. Instead, we should have confidence in Him and His Word.

The Apostle John testified, "There is no fear in love; but perfect love casts out fear, because fear involves torment. But he who fears has not been made perfect in love" (1 John 4:18). If we abide in close fellowship with God—walking by faith, walking in the light, walking in the Spirit—all fears will subside.

Keep Walking in the Truth

Again, as we observed before in 2 Thessalonians 2:6-7, the Church has a restraining influence on the work of Satan. The indwelling

> *In God's sovereign plan, the Church helps prevent Satan from moving into his end game.*

ministry of the Holy Spirit within the Body of Christ keeps Satan from having more influence in the world than he otherwise would. In God's sovereign plan, the Church helps prevent Satan from moving into his end game.

The New Testament repeatedly challenges believers not to be deceived. The term *deceive* (planao) literally means to be led astray or to wander away. Notice how the word is used in Scripture:

> Brethren, if anyone among you <u>wanders</u> from the truth, and someone turns him back, let him know that he who turns a sinner from the error of his way will save a soul from death and cover a multitude of sins (James 5:19-20).
>
> For you were like sheep going <u>astray,</u> but have now returned to the Shepherd and Overseer of your souls (1 Pet. 2:25).
>
> What do you think? If a man has a hundred sheep, and one of them goes <u>astray,</u> does he not leave the ninety-nine and go to the mountains to seek the one that is <u>straying</u>? (Matt. 18:12).

Falling into deception is, in fact, wandering or being led astray from the faith. This temptation is ever-present in this world, which underscores the importance of holding fast to the Word of God.

John 17 reveals a statement by our Savior that is germane to the discussion at hand. This powerful section of the Gospel of John displays the Lord Jesus praying to the Father shortly before He went to the cross. Referring to the disciples, Jesus stated, "Sanctify them by Your truth. Your word is truth" (John 17:17). God's Word is the only infallible and absolute standard of truth. We are to be, "sanctified by the truth" (John 17:19). It is the means by which we grow in our faith.

Earlier in the Gospel of John, the Apostle informs us, "Then Jesus said to those Jews who believed Him, 'If you abide in My word, you are My disciples indeed. And you shall know the truth, and the truth shall make you free'" (John 8:31-32). This text demonstrates the difference between a believer and a believer who is also a disciple of Christ. A student of Christ abides in His Word (truth). Abiding in God's truth keeps us from wandering into deception.

Satan has a plan for God's people. He wants them to fall into deception, and thereby keep them from being effective ambassadors for Christ.

Satan has a plan for God's people. He wants them to fall into deception, and thereby keep them from being effective ambassadors for Christ. This explains why there is always a steady attack on God's Word. When believers stray from the Bible, they play right into Satan's hand. The most important remedy for deception is knowledge of the truth. We must get into the Word of God regularly and stay there.

Always Remember Who Wins in the End

Our bodies have been deeply impacted by the fall of man into sin. Paul instructs, "Therefore, just as through one man sin entered the world, and death through sin, and thus death spread to all men, because all sinned" (Rom. 5:12). Christ was victorious over death when He rose from the grave. For believers in Christ, we will receive our new glorified bodies at the Rapture of the Church. Paul taught the Christians in Corinth:

For this corruptible must put on incorruption, and this mortal must put on immortality. So when this corruptible has put on incorruption, and this mortal has put on immortality, then shall be brought to pass the saying that is written: "Death is swallowed up in victory. O Death, where is your sting? O Hades, where is your victory?" (1 Cor. 15:53-55).

Believers no longer have to fear death because our future with Christ is secure. This glorious truth caused Paul to proclaim, "But thanks be to God, who gives us the victory through our Lord Jesus Christ" (1 Cor. 15:57).

It is important to keep the big picture in mind because it makes us less susceptible to deception in the present age. Things are seldom as they appear. The coming domination of this world by the Antichrist is intimidating. The work of Satan in this present world is expansive. If our focus is solely on what the forces of darkness will accomplish, we are only left with part of the story. It is critical to remember that in the end Christ will be victorious.

This takes us back to 2 Thessalonians 2:8 which teaches, "And then the lawless one will be revealed, whom the Lord will consume with the breath of His mouth and destroy with the brightness of His coming." Neither the Antichrist nor Satan will be any match for Christ in the end. It will not even be a contest.

The book of Revelation adds remarkable clarity and detail to our understanding of the future events of this world. It is there that we see how Christ will dispose of Satan and the Antichrist. Right now Satan is still allowed to have access to heaven. This will change halfway through the Tribulation:

So the great dragon was cast out, that serpent of old, called the Devil and Satan, who deceives the whole world; he was cast to the earth, and his angels were cast out with him. Then I heard a loud voice saying in heaven, "Now salvation, and strength, and the kingdom of our God, and the power of His Christ have come, for the accuser of our brethren, who accused them before our God day and night, has been cast down" (Rev. 12:9-10).

Revelation 19 brings us to the very end of the Tribulation, when the armies of the nations of the world will be gathered to fight with the armies of heaven. The Antichrist (the beast) will lead his forces into battle with Christ. It will not be much of a fight. The Apostle John recorded:

Then the beast was captured, and with him the false prophet who worked signs in his presence, by which he deceived those who received the mark of the beast and those who worshiped his image. These two were cast alive into the lake of fire burning with brimstone. And the rest were killed with the sword which proceeded from the mouth of Him who sat on the horse. And all the birds were filled with their flesh (Rev. 19:20-21).

The beast and the false prophet will be thrown into the lake of fire, which has been prepared for the Devil and his angels (Matt. 25:41). The armies of the nations will be killed by the spoken word of Christ. If this were a boxing match, the first punch would be a knockout blow.

Satan will also need to be dealt with. This is what comes next:

Then I saw an angel coming down from heaven, having the key to the bottomless pit and a great chain in his hand. He laid hold of the dragon, that serpent of old, who is the Devil and Satan, and bound him for a thousand years; and he cast him into the bottomless pit, and shut him up, and set a seal on him, so that he should deceive the nations no more till the thousand years were finished. But after these things he must be released for a little while (Rev. 20:1-3).

Satan will be held for a thousand years in the bottomless pit. During the Millennium, he will be unable to deceive the nations.

Revelation 20:3 indicates that Satan will not escape, but instead will be released after a thousand years. We again are told that he, "will go out to deceive the nations which are in the four corners of the earth, Gog and Magog, to gather them together to battle, whose number is as the sand of the sea" (Rev. 20:8). Satan will then be reunited with the Antichrist and the false prophet, "The devil, who deceived them, was cast into the lake of fire and brimstone where the beast and the false prophet are. And they will be tormented day and night forever and

The message of Revelation can be summed up in two words: God wins!

ever" (Rev. 20:10). The message of Revelation can be summed up in two words: God wins!

Be on Guard Because Things Will Get Worse

As bad as things are, never forget Paul's warning. Deception and evil men will continue to get worse and worse (2 Tim. 3:13). During the Tribulation things will be much worse than they have ever been. This is the teaching Paul revealed to the church at Thessalonica, "The coming of the lawless one is according to the working of Satan, with all power, signs, and lying wonders, and with all unrighteous deception among those who perish" (2 Thess. 2:9-10). The deceptive power of the Antichrist represents an increase in intensity, when compared with Satan's deceptive work in the present age.

In many ways, the arrival of the Antichrist will mimic the coming of Christ.

A closer look at 2 Thessalonians reveals a subtle truth about the arrival of the Antichrist. In verse 1 Paul specifically mentioned the subject at hand is the *coming* (parousia) of the Lord Jesus Christ. As the Apostle switched to the arrival of the Antichrist in verse 9, he also referred to his *coming* (parousia). In many ways, the arrival of the Antichrist will mimic the coming of Christ.

In Matthew 24 we learn that during the Tribulation many will claim to be the Christ. Jesus told His disciples, "For many will come in My name, saying, 'I am the Christ,' and will deceive many" (Matt. 24:5). False prophets will join in on the act, "Then many false prophets will rise up and deceive many" (Matt. 24:11). One man will actually stand in the Temple of God and demand to be worshipped (Matt. 24:15). The Antichrist will be seeking the worship that belongs to God alone. Therefore, it should not surprise us that much of what he will do is merely a cheap imitation of the Lord Jesus Christ. The Antichrist will try to pattern his outward appearance and arrival after the true Christ. Jesus continued to warn:

> Then if anyone says to you, "Look, here is the Christ!" or "There!" do not believe it. For false christs and false prophets will rise and show great signs and wonders to deceive, if possible, even the elect. See, I have told you beforehand. Therefore if they say to you, "Look, He is in the desert!" do not go out; or "Look, He is in the inner rooms!" do not believe it (Matt. 24:23-26).

By way of contrast, the Second Coming of Christ will be evident to the entire world (Matt. 24:27-31).

Believers in Christ need to be steadfast in their faith because Satan wants to devour Christians (1 Pet. 5:8-9). It should be a great comfort to know that *he can be resisted!* We must be vigilant in our faith and on guard for his attacks. We must be, "steadfast, immovable, always abounding in the work of the Lord, knowing that your labor is not in vain in the Lord" (1 Cor. 15:58).

Don't Wait! Today Is the Day of Salvation

2 Thessalonians 2:11-12 warns that for those who do not know Christ, a day is coming when they will reach the point of no return. As we have said, it will get harder and harder to trust Christ as time goes on. One of Satan's top priorities is to keep the lost, lost.

For those people left behind after the Rapture, if they were blinded by Satan's deception in the present Church Age, imagine how hard it will be to overcome an even greater deceptive power under the sway of the Antichrist! This underscores the importance of responding to the truth of Christ today.

The bad news is that our sin has a penalty, which is eternal separation from God in a literal place of torment called hell.

Have you ever trusted in Jesus Christ for eternal salvation? The reality is that every one of us is born a sinner. This is why the Bible teaches, "For all have sinned and fall short of the glory of God" (Rom. 3:23). Each of us has fallen short of God's standard of perfection. The bad news is that our sin has a penalty, which is eternal separation from God in a literal place of torment called hell. No amount of good works can take care of our sin problem. Entrance into heaven requires perfect righteousness.

The good news is that God has given us a gift, out of His love for us. The Bible teaches, "But God demonstrates His own love toward us, in that while we were still sinners, Christ died for us" (Rom. 5:8). God provided for our salvation when He sent His Son, Jesus, to die in our place on the cross. Jesus' work on the cross paid the penalty for our sin. This most certainly is good news.

> All who trust Jesus Christ, the Son of God, and Him alone, to forgive their sins and give them the free gift of eternal life will be saved.

The grace of God has provided mankind with hope. All who trust Jesus Christ, the Son of God, and Him alone, to forgive their sins and give them the free gift of eternal life will be saved. God wanted people to be rescued by the death and resurrection of His Son. This is why He wrote it down in His Word and told us, "But as many as received Him, to them He gave the right to become children of God, to those who believe in His name" (John 1:12). The message of the good news of Jesus Christ and His work on the cross saves those who believe it. When we believe the gospel message, Christ's perfect righteousness covers our sin and grants us entrance into heaven.

It is dangerous to put off this decision. Every day people depart from this world unexpectedly. Let me encourage you to trust in what Jesus has done on the cross for you. It is all you will ever need to take away the penalty of your sins, and assure you a place in heaven. Today is the day of salvation!

Discussion Questions – Chapter 9

1. What is the danger of fear?

2. How should Christians live, if not in fear?

3. What effect does the Church have on the work of Satan?

4. Describe what will keep us from wandering into deception.

5. In what way has Christ already been victorious? How will He be victorious in the future?

6. Describe the progression of the battle between Christ and Satan, as presented in Revelation.

7. How will the arrival of the Antichrist mimic the coming of Christ? What is Satan's purpose in this?

8. As we live in this present age, what actions do believers need to take?

9. If you are not a Christian, what action do you need to take?

Conclusion

Things are not always as they appear. We live in a frightening world of deception and hidden agendas. It is a world of spiritual realities, cosmic battles, unseen enemies, and demonic principalities. When we wake up to the world as it really is, it can be terrifying. Yet, wake up we must if we are to survive this great last days deception. Thankfully, we have a Savior who promised never to leave us or forsake us.

In God's Word we have everything we need for life and godliness. He has given us a blueprint for living that allows us to overcome Satan's deceptive agenda if we will simply walk in the truth. Satan's human envoys, the Luciferian elite, are no match for our Savior who has overcome death, hell and the grave. Although things are getting worse and worse in this present evil age, the final outcome has already been determined. God wins!

Believers in Jesus Christ have much to be thankful for. God has equipped us with everything we need to keep us from falling into deception. Our eternal life is secure in His Son, Jesus Christ. As part of the Church, we will be rescued before that great and awful Day of the Lord, when the Antichrist will wreak havoc on the world. There is exceptional peace and comfort from knowing God.

Because we know that the spirit of the Antichrist is already at work in the world, it is harder for Satan to advance his agenda.

Because we know that the spirit of the Antichrist is already at work in the world, it is harder for Satan to advance his agenda. We see him coming a mile away. When we walk in the light, it is impossible for the agents of darkness to be successful. Stay in the Word.

Study biblical doctrine. Research history. Look beyond the surface. Search out the truth. Examine everything through the lens of Scripture. Knowledge is a great defense against deception. Let us stand strong in the truth of Christ as we continue to be on guard against the great deception of these last days.

> You are all sons of light and sons of the day. We are not of the night nor of darkness. Therefore let us not sleep, as others do, but let us watch and be sober. For those who sleep, sleep at night, and those who get drunk are drunk at night. But let us who are of the day be sober, putting on the breastplate of faith and love, and as a helmet the hope of salvation. For God did not appoint us to wrath, but to obtain salvation through our Lord Jesus Christ, who died for us, that whether we wake or sleep, we should live together with Him. Therefore comfort each other and edify one another, just as you also are doing (1 Thess. 5:5–11).

If you need encouragement or if you would like more information about how to have eternal life, please contact the author at info@notbyworks.org.

Bibliography

Albrecht, Katherine and McIntyre, Liz. *Spychips: How Major Corporations and Government Plan to Track Your Every Purchase and Watch Your Every Move.* New York: Pengiun Group, 2006.

Allen, Gary. *None Dare Call It Conspiracy.* Cutchogue, NY: Buccaneer Books, 1976.

Bernays, Edward. *Propaganda.* Brooklyn, NY: IG Publishing, 1928.

Connet, Paul, Beck, James, and Micklem, H.S. *The Case Against Fluoride: How Hazardous Waste Ended Up in Our Drinking Water and the Bad Science and Powerful Politics That Keep It There.* White River Junction, VT: Chelsea Green Publishing, 2010.

Dice, Mark. *Big Brother: The Orwellian Nightmare Come True.* San Diego, CA: The Resistance, 2011.

Eakman, B. K. *Walking Targets: How Our Psychological Classrooms Are Producing a Nation of Sitting Ducks.* Raleigh, NC: Midnight Whistler Publishers, 2007.

Fruchtenbaum, Arnold G. *The Messianic Jewish Epistles: Hebrews, James, First Peter, Second Peter, Jude. 1st ed.* Tustin, CA: Ariel Ministries, 2005.

Gatto, John Taylor. *Weapons of Mass Instruction: A Schoolteacher's Journey Through the Dark World of Compulsory Schooling.* Gabriola Island, BC: New Society Publishers, 2010.

_____. *The Underground History of American Education: An Intimate Investigation into the Prison of Modern Schooling.* New York: Oxford Village Press, 2006.

Griffin, David Ray. *The New Pearl Harbor Revisited: 9/11, The Cover-up and the Exposé.* Northampton, MA: Olive Branch Press, 2008.

Griffin, G. Edward. *The Creature From Jekyll Island.* Westlake Village, CA: American Media, 1994.

Gromacki, Robert. *Stand Bold in Grace: An Exposition of Hebrews.* The Gromacki Expository Series. The Woodlands, TX: Kress Christian Publications, 2002.

Henry, Carl F. H. "Postmodernism: The New Spectre?" In *The Challenge of Postmodernism: An Evangelical Engagement,* ed. David S. Dockery. Wheaton, IL: Victor Books, 1995.

Hiebert, D. Edmond. *Everyman's Bible Commentary: First Timothy.* Chicago, IL: Moody Press, 1957.

Isberyt, Charlotte Thomson. *The Deliberate Dumbing Down of America.* Ravenna, OH: Conscience Press, 1999.

Jeffrey, Grant R. *Shadow Government: How the Secret Global Elite Is Using Surveillance Against You.* Colorado Springs, CO: Waterbrook Press, 2009.

Kah, Gary H. *The Demonic Roots of Globalism.* Lafayette, LA: Vital Issues Press, 1995.

Kent, Homer Jr. *The Epistle to the Hebrews: A Commentary.* Winona Lake, IN: BMH Books, 2002.

Koehler, Ludwig, Walter Baumgartner, M. E. J. Richardson, and Johann Jakob Stamm. *The Hebrew and Aramaic Lexicon of the Old Testament.* Leiden, New York: E.J. Brill, 1999.

Marrs, Jim. *The Rise of the Fourth Reich: The Secret Societies That Threaten to Take Over America.* New York: HarperCollins, 2008.

——————. *Rule By Secrecy.* New York: William Morrow, 2001.

Miller, Stephen R. Vol. 18, *Daniel. The New American Commentary.* Nashville, TN: Broadman & Holman Publishers, 1994.

Monteith, Stanley. *Brotherhood of Darkness*. Oklahoma City, OK: Hearthstone Publishing, LTD, 2000.

Napolitano, Andrew P. *Lies the Government Told You*. Nashville: Thomas Nelson, 2010.

Quigley, Carroll. *Tragedy and Hope: A History of the World in Our Time*. New York: McMillan, 1966.

Radmacher, Earl D., Ronald Barclay Allen, and H. Wayne House. *Nelson's New Illustrated Bible Commentary*. Nashville, TN: T. Nelson Publishers, 1999.

Rothkopf, David. *Superclass: The Global Power Elite and the World They Are Making*. New York: Farrar, Straus and Giroux, 2008.

Ryrie, Charles Caldwell. *Basic Theology: A Popular Systematic Guide to Understanding Biblical Truth*. Chicago, IL: Moody Press, 1999.

Skousen, W. Cleon. *The Naked Capitalist*. Cutchogue, NY: Buccaneer Books, 1970.

Springmeier, Fritz. *Bloodlines of the Illuminati*. Pentracks Publications, 2007.

Stormer, John A. *None Dare Call It Education: The Documented Account of How Education "Reforms" Are Undermining Academics and Traditional Values*. Florissant, MO: Liberty Bell Press, 1999.

Sutton, Antony C. *America's Secret Establishment: An Introduction to the Order of Skull & Bones*. Walterville, OR: Trineday, LLC, 2009.

Tarpley, Webster Griffin. *9/11 Synthetic Terror: Made in USA, Fifth Edition*. Joshua Tree, CA: Progressive Press, 2006.

Turtel, Joel. *Public Schools, Public Menace: How Public Schools Lie to Parents and Betray Our Children*. Staten Island, NY: Liberty Books, 2005.

Ventura, Jesse and Russell, Dick. *63 Documents the Government Doesn't Want You to Read*. New York: Skyhorse Publishing, 2011.

Wakefield, Andrew J. *Callous Disregard: Autism and Vaccines—The Truth Behind a Tragedy*. New York: Skyhorse Publishing, 2010.

Watson, Paul Joseph. "Bill Gates: Use Vaccines to Lower Population." http://www.infowars.com/bill-gates-use-vaccines-to-lower-population/.

Wilson, Woodrow. *The New Freedom: A Call For the Emancipation of the Generous Energies of a People*, 1913.

Wolf, Naomi. *The End of America: Letter of Warning to a Young Patriot*. White River Junction, VT, Chelsea Green Publishing, 2007.

CPSIA information can be obtained
at www.ICGtesting.com
Printed in the USA
FFOW01n1324280714
6515FF